D. P. Madison

Some American Ladies

Seven Informal Biographies

Martha Washington
Abigail Adams   Dolly Madison
Elizabeth Monroe   Louisa Adams   Rachel Jackson
Peggy Eaton

By

Meade Minnigerode

With 16 Illustrations

G. P. Putnam's Sons
New York & London
The Knickerbocker Press
1926

Made in the United States of America

For

ROGER SHERMAN

OF RYE

CONTENTS

PAGE

MARTHA WASHINGTON 1

ABIGAIL ADAMS 47

DOLLY MADISON 89

ELIZABETH MONROE AND LOUISA ADAMS 133

RACHEL JACKSON 183

PEGGY EATON 241

v

ILLUSTRATIONS

FACING
PAGE

DOLLY MADISON . . . . . *Frontispiece*
From an engraving by John Sartain.

MARTHA WASHINGTON 16
From an engraving by Buttre.

GEORGE WASHINGTON 32
From an engraving published in 1784 by Whitworth and Yates.

ABIGAIL ADAMS 64
From the painting by Stuart.

JOHN ADAMS 80
From an engraving published in 1783 by J. Fielding.

THE BURNING OF WASHINGTON IN 1814 124

THE PRESIDENT'S HOUSE IN 1814 128
From an engraving published in 1814 by G. and S. Robinson.

ELIZABETH MONROE 140
From an engraving by Buttre.

THE ENTRY OF NAPOLEON INTO PARIS FROM ELBA IN 1815 160
From a contemporary American print.

LOUISA ADAMS 176
From an engraving by Storm.

RACHEL JACKSON 200
From an engraving by Buttre.

vii

FACING
PAGE

ANDREW JACKSON 216
From a contemporary print.

RACHEL JACKSON 232
From a contemporary print.

PEGGY EATON 256
From a portrait by Inman. Courtesy of the Robert
Fridenberg Galleries.

THE PRESIDENT'S HOUSE IN 1831 272
From an engraving published in 1831 by Hinton, Simpkin
& Marshall.

MARTIN VAN BUREN 280
From an engraving of a portrait by Inman.

Some American Ladies

Martha Washington

MARTHA WASHINGTON

1

IT is said that a cantankerous old Scotchman once informed George Washington that he would have been nobody at all if he had not married the widow Custis. On the other hand, it is doubtful whether any-one beyond her immediate, contemporary circle would ever have heard of the widow Custis if she had not decided to marry George Washington.

She was born on June 21, 1731, in New Kent County, Virginia; Martha, the oldest of several brothers and sisters, children of Colonel John Dandridge and his wife Frances Jones. It was a well connected family, scholars and divines on the mother's side, planter officials on the father's who was himself County Clerk. They lived quite elegantly and fashionably on the Pamunkey, not far from Williamsburg. There, in the pleasant, hospitable, decorously sophisticated atmosphere of Colonial Virginia—although some thought it depraved and extravagantly worldly—Martha was brought up; a brown haired, hazel eyed girl, very slim and short, quick spirited and perhaps a little sharp with her tongue, for whom the pantries, and kitchens, and sewing rooms held no mysteries. She was very devout, she played on the spinnet, she embroidered and knitted, she danced, and she rode horseback to hounds. As with other Virginia damsels of her day, her education did not greatly concern itself with other matters; she was trained to be an efficient housekeeper, the mistress of some well ordered future home, and a gracefully decorative figure at routs and assemblies. Provided these ends were achieved, it was not esteemed a question of any moment whether she learned much else.

But in her fifteenth year she was queening it as a belle at Williamsburg, making her curtsey to Governor Gooch at the Palace, and attracting her share of attention and masculine admiration. Williamsburg —with its sandy streets laid out in the form of a W and M in honor of its royal patrons, William and Mary—was the capital of Virginia; the great gathering place of lawyers, officials and scholars; the social centre of the Colony. There were gay times at Williamsburg, in the mansions of the Pages, and Raes, and Fairfaxes, and Barradalls, and when they all drove up in their coaches along the avenue of catalpa trees to the Governor's House to dance in the mirrored candlelight, a brilliant pageant of jewelled brocades and powdered heads. Life was never more stately and amenable, society, graced with the pomp

and courtliness of the Royal Governors, can never
have appeared more enduring and seemly, than in
those last decades of the Colonial régime. Those were
English ladies and gentlemen—Lords and Ladies
some of them—whose sons were sent overseas to
school, who lived on their Virginia estates as they
might have in their home counties and shires; for
whom their sojourn at Williamsburg must reproduce as closely as possible the elegance and gaiety of
London and Bath.

Martha Dandridge moved in this society, very correct, admirably discreet, sufficiently sprightly. She
had a retinue of beaux, but soon there was only one
that mattered. He was nearly twice her age, Daniel
Parke Custis, the son of Colonel John Custis and
Frances Parke, whose father had been "Captain
Generall and Chief Governor of the Leeward
Islands." He was a handsome young man, of good
family and considerable wealth, and he should long
before have married his cousin Evelyn Byrd—had
either of them been disposed to obey parental dic-
tates—so that at first there was opposition on Colonel
Custis's part to his son's suit; but in time the Colonel
came to have "so good a character of her," a friend
wrote Daniel about Martha, "that he had rather you
should have her than any lady in Virginia—nay, if
possible, he is as much enamoured with her character
as you are with her person." However, it would be

best for Daniel to "hurry down immediately for fear
he should change the strong inclination he has to your
marrying directly."

And so they were married, in June, 1749, at St.
Peter's church in New Kent County.

2

There followed eight happy years—except for the
death of two sons in early childhood—spent at Mr.
Custis's home, the White House, on the York, or at
the Six Chimney House at Williamsburg. Two other
children, Martha and John Parke—Patsy and Jackey
—survived; the Custises lived quietly on their country estate, or took occasional part in the social festivities of Governor Dinwiddie's era; Mr. Custis was
appointed Crown Councilor, but was prevented by
the delicacy of his health from taking up his office.
More and more, probably, they would have sought
the peaceful retirement of the White House; the
years would have passed in inconspicuous content-
ment; the world, perhaps Williamsburg itself, would
have forgotten Martha Dandridge Custis.

But in the spring of 1757 Mr. Custis died, and
Martha was a widow at twenty-six. Alone in her
home with two small children, and the wealthiest
widow in Virginia—sole executrix of a large landed
estate, including the two houses, and mistress of an
important fortune, forty-five thousand pounds ster-

ling of which she held in trust for the children. It must have been a perplexing responsibility, but Martha assumed it without hesitation, and with the aid of her stewards and agents, under the guidance of her friend Mr. Robert Nicholas, she gave her personal, and thoroughly competent, attention to the administration of her property. A charming young widow—little Patsy Custis, for she was "Patsy" too —so capable and self-reliant, and so rich. It was not any later than necessary that the suitors came riding along the red Virginia roads, up to the portals of the White House in which she now permanently resided.

Except on those occasions when she escaped to a neighbor's for a few days to avoid their importunities. At all events, in May, 1758, she was at the home of her friends the Chamberlaynes, and it seemed that in this instance Martha had only jumped out of the frying pan into the fire. For one morning her host went down to William's Ferry, opposite the house, to greet a friend who was passing through to Williamsburg on urgent business. It was most urgent business, but Major Chamberlayne argued with him, and told him that the widow Custis was at the house, and prevailed upon him to stay for dinner. But only for dinner. They came in to the parlor, and when Martha saw the guest it was young Colonel George Washington.

She had probably met him already at Williamsburg, perhaps in 1754 when all Virginia was ringing
with the name of its military hero; she certainly did
not need to be told who he was, or that he had had two
horses shot under him and four bullets through his
coat with Braddock.   Now she saw him before her,
tall, distinguished, most elegant and dignified.   They
were both of them most elegant and dignified.   Enormously dignified.   She was not quite twenty-seven, he
was a little past twenty-six.   He stayed for dinner; he
stayed all afternoon he finally stayed overnight.   It
was not too early the next morning when he rode
off to Williamsburg on that urgent business. A little
while later he was back again, visiting Martha at the
White House, and this time when he left they were
engaged.   It had been love at first sight, so people
said.

He was gone all summer with the expedition
against Fort Duquesne, and in July he wrote to her
that he embraced the opportunity—

"to send a few words to one whose life is now insepa-
rable from mine. Since that happy hour when we
made our pledges to each other, my thoughts have
been continually going to you as to another Self. That
All-powerful Providence may keep us both in safety
is the prayer of your faithful and ever affectionate
friend."

It was a love letter, a love letter from dignified George.

They were married on January 6, 1759, at the White House—some say at St. Peter's—before a tremendous gathering of friends and relatives. He was in blue and silver trimmed with scarlet, with gold buckles; she wore a white satin quilted petticoat under an overskirt of white corded silk shot with silver; there were pearls in her hair and diamonds on her slippers. Patsy and George. After the wedding Martha drove in a coach and six with liveried postilions to the Six Chimney House at Williamsburg— Colonel Washington was a member of the House of Burgesses and his duties were to keep them there for several months—while the bridegroom rode alongside with an escort of gentlemen. Perhaps with all her wedding finery there was not room for two in the coach. . . .

3

It had been love at first sight, so people said, but Martha was not George's first love, nor his third, nor yet his fifth; nor was she ever, perhaps, his real love.

He had been a very rejected lover ever since the age of fifteen, and Martha herself must have known it. Frances Alexander, first, for whom he composed an acrostic. Then Betsy Fauntleroy, to whose father he wrote that he proposed to "wait on Miss

Betsy in hopes of the revocation of the former cruel
sentence and see if I can meet with any alteration in
my favor." But there was no alteration, and he
turned next to his cousin Lucy Grymes, who with
Miss Fauntleroy is supposed to have been the "Low
Land Beauty" of his correspondence. They were
both great Tidewater belles, and they both preferred
other suitors.

"I pass the time much more agreeably than I
imagined I should," he wrote to a friend during this
period, "as there is a very agreeable young lady lives
in the same house where I reside that in a great measure cheats sorrow and dejectedness, though not so
as to draw my thoughts altogether from your parts."
And to another friend he reported that she was very
agreeable, "but as that's only adding fuel to fire, it
makes me the more uneasy, for by often, and un-
avoidably, being in company with her revives my
former passion for your Low Land Beauty; whereas,
was I to live more retired from young women, I
might in some measure eliviate my sorrows by bury-
ing that chaste and troublesome passion in the grave
of oblivion or etarnall forgetfulness; for as I am very
well assured, that's the only antidote or remedy that
I shall ever be relieved by or only recess that can
administer any cure or help to me, as I am well
convinced, was I ever to attempt any thing, I should
only get a denial which would be only adding grief
to uneasiness."

The lady in question was Mary Cary—the sister of Sally Cary Fairfax, wife of his friend and neighbor Colonel George Fairfax of Belvoir—and for a while George thought that he was in love with her too. Then, in 1757, it was Mary Philipse of Yonkers, whom he met while on a visit to New York, but he did not exert himself particularly to gain her favor, and she fulfilled her destiny which was to marry Colonel Roger Morris and become the mistress of the future Jumel mansion. One after the other, the young officer had experienced these always unfortunate passions, and Martha must surely have been aware of them. What she would not have known was that most of them were makeshift, substitute affairs, however acute at the moment, and that George was actually desperately in love with an entirely different lady.

It was Sally Cary and he had been in love with her before her marriage, but her father had reminded him that she was "accustomed to her coach and six." The young man who was eventually to ride in one of the most beautiful coaches in the country could not afford one then, and Sally married Colonel Fairfax, but George was never to forget her. She was two years older than he, a very intelligent, cultured and altogether charming lady, who, after her marriage, continued her friendship for him and served, in some measure, as a tutor to him in refinement and deportment during his less polished years. Whether she was in love with him is not, at the present time, manifest. She was a person of rare discretion, and Colonel Fairfax was never known to resent her slightest actions. That George Washington was still deeply in love with her can not be doubted, but he, too, was a person of exceptional restraint and self-control, and one is to believe that she never suspected it—until he told her.

For he told her, finally, in September, 1758, some three months before his marriage to Martha Custis, to whom his thoughts had supposedly been continually going that summer, "as to another Self." He had been corresponding with Sally Fairfax—a renewal of correspondence which was to make him "happier than the day is long" he had assured her in 1755, although she had desired news from him to be "communicated in a letter to somebody of your acquaintance," prudent lady—and at last he had to tell her. For once there was an end to restraint, but not to dignity.

"Dear Madam," he wrote, "yesterday I was honored with your short but very agreeable favor. . . . How joyfully I catch the happy occasion of renewing a correspondence which I fear'd was disrelish'd on your part. . . . In silence I now express my joy. Silence which in some cases—I wish the present—speaks more intelligibly than the sweetest eloquence.

If you allow that any honor can be deriv'd from my opposition to our present system of management"— this is doubtless a reference to military affairs—"you destroy the merit of it entirely in me by attributing my anxiety to the animating prospect of possessing Mrs. Custis, when I need not name it, guess yourself, should not my own honor and country's welfare be the incitement.

" 'Tis true I profess myself a votary to love. I acknowledge that a lady is in the case, and, further, I confess that this lady is known to you. Yes, Madam, as well as she is to one who is too sensible of her charms to deny the power whose influence he feels and must ever submit to. I feel the force of her amiable beauties in recollection of a thousand passages that I would wish to obliterate till I am bid to revive them; but experience, alas, sadly reminds me how impossible this is and evinces an opinion which I have long entertained that there is a destiny which has the sovereign control of our actions, not to be resisted by the strongest efforts of human nature.

"You have drawn me, dear Madam, or rather I have drawn myself into an honest confession of a simple fact. Misconstrue not my meaning, 'tis obvious; doubt it not, nor expose it"—she never did, and it remained for biographers to betray him— "The world has no business to know the object of my love declared in this manner to you when I want to conceal it. One thing above all things in this world I wish to know, and only one person of your acquaintance can solve me that or guess my meaning; but adieu to this till happier times, if I ever shall see them;

the hours at present are melancholy dull. . . . I
dare believe you are happy as you say. I wish I was
happy too."

He wished he was happy too, in September, this
young man who in May had fallen in love at first
sight with Martha Custis, and won her hand. One
begins to understand—that frigid little love letter
to Patsy in July, the empty seat in the coach on that
wedding day in January. With Sally Fairfax in
mind, one wonders what took place at Major Chamberlayne's and later at the White House. What did
he see there—an attractive young widow blessed
with worldly goods, graced with qualities which made
her in every way suited to be his wife, since he must
inevitably marry someone. And Martha, with her
business cares and her two small children, it was
inevitable that she should marry again. One imagines
that they understood each other perfectly.

That for long years George and Martha Washington shared each others' lives, in complete serenity
and sympathy, and with ever increasing affection and
devotion, remains perhaps his greatest and most
admirable achievement, her most noteworthy accom-
plishment. For he never forgot Sally Fairfax. She
went back to England in 1773, and when her husband
died, in 1787, she remained there and finished her days
at Bath. And in 1798—forty years after his marriage, one year and seven months before his death—

George Washington wrote to the lady he had not seen for twenty-five years. He wondered why, he had "wondered often, your nearest relations being in this country, that you should not prefer spending the evening of your life among them rather than close the sublunary scene in a foreign country." And he related the events of the intervening years to her, none of which, however——

". . . nor all of them together, have been able to eradicate from my mind the recollections of those happy moments—*the happiest in my life*—which I have enjoyed in your company. . . ."

4

That was in 1798—but in 1759 Colonel Washington had just taken a wife, and there was married life, and all the future, to be faced. They stayed at Williamsburg for the session of the House, and then they went to Mount Vernon; Martha and George, and the two Custis children whom their childless stepfather always treated as though they had been his own. Delicate children, Patsy and Jackey, who caused their mother much anxiety.

"My dear Nancy," she once wrote to one of her sisters, "I had the pleasure to receive your kind letter . . . just as I was setting out on a visit to Mr. Washington in Westmoreland whare I spent a weak very agreabley. I carred my little patt"—Patsy—"with

me and left Jackey at home for a trial to see how well
I coud stay without him; though we ware gon but
won fortnight I was quite impatient to get home.
. . . We all injoy very good health at preasent, I
think patty seems to be quite well now, Jackey is
very thin but in good health, and learn thaire books
very fast. . . . If I coud leave my children in as
good Care as you can I would never let Mr. W—n
come down without me—" to the sessions at Williamsburg, she meant, which he attended, sometimes without her, in the winter.

Little Patsy was well then, but as she grew up
into the brunette "dark lady" so beloved of that countryside, it was quite apparent that her health was
declining; the Virginia Warm Springs did no good
—and in June, 1773, she died. And Jackey's health
improved, but as he approached young manhood he
was hard to manage; he would not pay attention to
his books in the school at Annapolis, he was filled with
notions of a European tour, and when they sent him
to King's College in New York he was not contented.
And the real reason was that he was in love with little
Nellie Calvert, of Mount Airy, and so, finally, in
February, 1774, they were married and went to live
on his estate of Abingdon on the Potomac. It was
not quite a year since Patsy's death, and Martha
did not attend the wedding, but she wrote to her
daughter-in-law.

MARTHA WASHINGTON

From an engraving by Buttre

"My dear Nellie—God took from Me a Daughter when June Roses were blooming— He has now given me another daughter, about her Age, when Winter winds are blowing, to warm my Heart again. I am as Happy as One so Afflicted and so Blest can be. Pray receive my Benediction and a wish that you may long live the Loving Wife of my happy Son, and a Loving Daughter of your Affectionate Mother. M. Washington."

Hers was always a great dignity, tempered with sweetness and grace. . . .

5

There were fifteen happy years at Mount Vernon, in the Mansion House among the farms, and if Martha could have had her way they would never have been interrupted. She was extremely busy—her negroes, her cows, two hundred of them, her gardening, her needlework, her charities, her housekeeping—a mode of life, simple, prosperous and dignified, eminently suited to her tastes and capacities. The Colonel was an enthusiastic gentleman farmer, she was an ideal gentleman farmer's wife, content to lead the well ordered, generously fed, elegantly clothed—for the Colonel was always in the fashion—and ceaselessly hospitable existence of that hunting, dining, crop raising Virginia countryside; and to ride abroad, when her own guests gave her time, in her coach and four behind the white and scarlet liveried postilions.

To Greenway Court, and to Gunston Hall, and to
Belvoir where Sally Fairfax still reigned so pleasantly. . . .

But it was not to last. There was trouble brewing
in the Colonies; Mr. Patrick Henry was making
speeches; Governor Dunmore was behaving insup-
portably; at Mount Vernon, Martha was fashioning
cotton dresses striped with silk from the ravellings
of old stockings and damask chair covers, while sixteen spinning wheels were constantly whirring in
order to replace the imported goods which England
wished to tax. And in September, 1774, Colonel
Washington was on his way to the Congress at Philadelphia. But Martha seemed——

"ready to make any sacrifice," Edmund Pendleton
wrote, "and was cheerful though I know she felt
anxious. . . . 'I hope you will all stand firm—I
know George will,' she said. The dear little woman
was busy from morning until night with domestic
duties, but she gave us much time in conversation and
affording us entertainment. When we set off in the
morning she stood in the door and cheered us with
the good words 'God be with you, gentlemen!'"

If things went wrong, if there was war with all its
dangers of pillage and confiscation, Martha had more
to lose, perhaps, than any woman in the Colonies except Mary Morris of Philadelphia, but "what are all
these evils," she said, "when compared with the fate

of which the Port Bill may be only a threat? My mind is made up, my heart is in the cause." So, quite simply and with a rare, unconscious courage, those Colonial ladies—Martha Washington, Abigail Adams, all of them—faced the future. And in June, 1775, there was a letter from the Colonel.

"My dearest—I now sit down to write you on a subject which fills me with inexpressible concern, and this concern is greatly aggravated and increased when I reflect upon the uneasiness I know it will give you. It has been determined in Congress that the whole army raised for the defence of the American cause shall be put under my care. . . . You may believe me, my dear Patsy, when I assure you . . . that . . . I have used every endeavor to avoid it . . . I shall feel no pain from the toil or the danger of the Campaign; my unhappiness will flow from the uneasiness you will feel from being left alone. I therefore beg that you will summon your whole fortitude, and pass your time as agreeably as possible."

At Mount Vernon, they wanted her to seek shelter inland, and she did pack her valuables and papers, but she said, "No, I will not desert my post." But in November, with Jackey and his wife, "the Lady of His Excellency General Washington" was off to the headquarters at Cambridge, at the invitation of the Commander in Chief. It was a noteworthy journey, made in considerable state, fraught with many courtesies on the way, solemnized by ceremonies of welcome and the military splendors of such picked bodies as the First Troop, Philadelphia City Cavalry. Plump, bonny little Patsy was become "Lady Washington." And at Cambridge the General was in hot water over questions of social etiquette—already— but Martha smoothed everything out at once, and gave pleasant parties for the young officers, and made some lifelong friends—Mrs. Knox, Mrs. Warren— for herself.

"I think the Complacency of her manners," Mrs. Warren told Mrs. John Adams, "speaks at once the benevolence of her heart, and her affability, Candor and gentleness qualify her to soften the hours of private life, or to sweeten the cares of the Hero, and smooth the rugged paths of War."

6

From then on, Martha was almost always in camp with the army in its winter quarters, returning to Mount Vernon when the spring brought on a resumption of warfare; with an occasional trip to Philadelphia, as in 1776 to be inoculated, when the Hancocks invited her to "take the small pox" at their house, a hospitality which she did not put to the final test. She always insisted afterwards that the sound of fifes and drums was pleasanter music than any

which she had ever heard. And once, in six years, the
General spent three days in his own home, on his
way to Yorktown.

There can be no question in these pages of taking
more than a glimpse at these encampments of the
Revolutionary War. What impresses one perhaps
most strongly is the fun which they managed to get
out of them. There was a society, there were dinners
and parties, there was horseback riding, there were
beautiful ladies, there was dancing. The General
once danced with fat Mrs. Knox for three continuous hours at one of those "pretty little frisks"—
High Betty Martin, no doubt, and Leather the
Strap, and Pettycoatee. There were reviews and
"genteel entertainments" for visiting foreigners and
Indian chiefs, who appeared to Martha—the Indians
—"like cutthroats all." There was also a vast amount
of knitting and mending for the soldiers, in which
Martha always took the lead; she enjoyed the rides
with her "old man" as she did not hesitate to call
him; and occasionally there were regular receptions
at headquarters, all "according to the ceremonial"—
for the simplest matters had to be attended to cere-
moniously always at the General's.

Morristown, even Valley Forge—where the officers
and men lived "chiefly in Hutts which they say is tolerable comfortable," and where Martha, and Mrs.
Knox, and Mrs. Biddle, and Lady Stirling shared

the rigors of that dreariest of winters—they always had a good time. Especially at Morristown, where Lady Stirling, and the Boudinots, and Mrs. John Morton entertained bevies of young ladies—the Misses Livingston, Lady Kitty, Betsy Schuyler, a great favorite of Martha's—who in turn entertained eager detachments of young officers, and among them Colonel Hamilton whenever Miss Betsy was of the party. Only the second winter at Morristown was rather uncomfortable for Martha. There were all the aides, and the family who owned the house, and *eighteen* servants, and it was extremely crowded; particularly when there was an alarm in the middle of the night and the Life Guards came rushing in, five of them at the opened window of every room, while Martha shivered under her inadequate quilts. . . .

And then it was Yorktown, but in the home in which there should have been the deepest joy there was only sorrow. For Jackey was desperately ill at Eltham of a fever caught in the camp, and Martha, with Mrs. Custis, was only just in time to reach him before he died, on November 5, 1781. He left four children, the two youngest of whom were adopted by the Washingtons and taken to Mount Vernon—little George Washington, and two year old Eleanor, the Nellie Custis of later presidential days. But there was hardly any time for private sorrows. A few weeks later Martha was with the General at Philadelphia, at the home of Benjamin Chew, in a city glittering with illuminations, uproarious with festivals and public functions; and in March, 1782, surrounded by the City Troop, they left for Newburgh.

There again, except for Martha who devoted herself to gardening, there was gaiety and "frisking," however crowded and confused. Parties and dances at Mrs. Knox's, dinners at headquarters, and that great affair at West Point in honor of the Dauphin of France; a review and fireworks, which the General and Lady Washington, with a distinguished company of guests, went to in a barge festooned with laurel; a ceremony followed by a banquet for five hundred persons, and that ball at which the General, "with a dignified and graceful air, having Mrs. Knox for his partner, carried down a dance of twenty couple in the arbor on the green grass."

And then, at last, it was December, 1783, and they were at Annapolis. There were magnificent festivities and a ball, and the next day, in the presence of many ladies gathered around Martha in the gallery of the Senate Chamber at the State House, the General placed his commission in the hands of Mr. Mifflin, President of the Congress. The Washingtons reached Mount Vernon on the evening of December 24; it was Christmas, the war was over, and they were home.

"Such a racket the servants made. . . . All Christmas afternoon people came to pay their Respects and Duty. Among them were stately Dames and gay young Women. The Gen'l seemed very happy, and Mistress Washington was from Day-brake making everything as agreeable as possible for everybody."

But now Sally Fairfax was not at Belvoir any more. . . .

7

Mount Vernon—but one can only stay for a moment.

A glance at the familiar silhouette of that hospitable mansion which the General at this period compared to a "well resorted tavern," so perpetually crowded was it with visitors of every station; a smile for General Lafayette's French hounds, who, "if they discovered no great disposition for hunting in the field," at least "so distinguished themselves in the kitchen that one of their number carried off a fine ham;" an agreeable picture of Nellie Custis and her young companions, frisking—it seems to have been the word—around her august grandfather; of Martha, dignified and affable, contentedly engrossed in her housekeeping; of the General, presiding in full dress at the head of his "good but not ostentatious" table, in the midst of a gathering which was a little inclined, perhaps, to idolize him, to treat him as though he had not been merely a simple, Virginia country gentleman at heart—until he became, and Martha with him, just a trifle obsessed himself with the awe which he inspired.

And then it was April, 1789, and the Secretary of Congress was at the door to tell them that the General was chosen to be President. "My movements to the chair of government," he wrote to General Knox, "will be accompanied by feelings not unlike those of a culprit who is going to the place of his execution." As for Martha,

"I little thought when the war was finished," she exclaimed, "that any circumstances could possibly happen which would call the General into public life again. I had anticipated that . . . we should be suffered to grow old together, in solitude and tranquility . . . I will not, however, contemplate with too much regret disappointments that were inevitable."

She was resigned to grandeur.

One wonders what Sally Fairfax thought of it all when she heard the news. She was pleased, one may be sure of that—even Lord Cornwallis was pleased, and sent his felicitations to his old enemy—she was pleased, and, one imagines, very proud. Proud of George, whom she had once befriended and advised; proud of Virginia; a little proud of herself, to think that she might have been riding in a coach and six to

be the very first First Lady in the land of her girlhood. But now it was Martha who rode in the coach
that May with her two grandchildren, through Philadelphia and Trenton—another gala day for the First
Troop—to the ferry at New York, where they were
waiting for her with the same state barge which had
conveyed her husband across to the city a few weeks
before. A tremendous barge, fifty feet long, festooned with red satin, and rowed by thirteen pilots
dressed in white and blue.

There was a cheerful din of welcoming guns and
bells, and they drove through the rather poorly paved
streets to the Franklin mansion on Cherry Street,
where there were Turkish carpets and "the greatest
quantity of plate and china I ever saw."

8

Martha was not to be very happy at New York,
either in her Franklin mansion or in the even more
imposing McComb residence on Broadway to which
they moved in 1790.

"I live a very dull life hear," she wrote, "and know
nothing that passes in the town—I never goe to any
public place—indeed I think I am more like a State
prisoner than anything else; there is a certain bounds
set for me which I must not depart from—and as I
cannot doe as I like, I am obstinate and stay at home
a great deal."

The President was quite ill in New York, and his mother died, so that there was no personal gaiety for them, and their official life was rigorously restricted; a state dinner to dignitaries once a week; his levees on Tuesday afternoons, at which he appeared in meticulous full dress with yellow gloves and a long sword in a white velvet scabbard; her receptions on Friday evenings, attended by a great number of "respectable characters"—Lady Mary Watts, Lady Kitty Duer, Lady Christiana Griffin, Mrs. Ralph Izard, Mrs. Theodore Sedgwick, Mrs. Livingston, Mrs. Alexander Hamilton—enormously decorous affairs, dare one say dull, rustling with silk and satin, colorful enough with bright Italian gauze scarves, decorated with ponderous globe shaped head-dresses trimmed with wreaths of roses as artificial as the hair which they adorned, sustained with plum cake and tea.

It was really not very gay. Of one dinner which he attended at the Mansion, Senator Maclay wrote that—

"It was the most solemn dinner ever I sat at. Not a health drank, scarce a word said until the cloth was taken away. Then the President filling a glass of wine with great formality drank to the health of every individual by name around the table. Everybody imitated him, charged glasses, and such a buzz of 'health Sir' and 'health Madam' and 'thank you Sir' and

'thank you Madam' never had I heard before. . . .
The ladies sat a good while and the bottles passed
about, but there was a dead silence almost. Mrs.
Washington at last withdrew with the ladies . . . I
expected the men would now begin, but the same still-
ness remained. The P told of a New England clergyman who had lost a hat and wig in passing a river
called the Brunks. He smiled and everybody else
laughed . . . We did not sit long after the ladies retired . . . I took my hat and came home."

It may have been the same dinner at which they
served the trifle made of sour cream, "on which the
General changed his plate immediately; but . . .
Mrs. Washington ate a whole heap of it."

Perhaps it was the fault of New York itself, where
in spite of a superficially brilliant society led by Mrs.
John Jay, few ladies—in the estimation of Miss Re-
becca Franks of Philadelphia, who was of course
prejudiced—knew how to entertain company in their
own houses "unless they introduce the card table."
In fact, with rare exceptions, she did not know—

"a woman or girl who can chat above half an hour.
. . . I will do our (Philadelphia) ladies the justice
to say that they have more cleverness in the turn of an
eye than those of New York have in their whole composition. With what ease have I seen a Chew, a Penn,
an Oswald, an Allen, and a thousand others, entertain a large circle of both sexes, the conversation,
without the aid of cards, never flagging nor seeming

in the least strained or stupid. Here"—in New York —"you enter the room with a formal set curtsey, and after the how-dos things are finished; all's a dead calm till the cards are introduced."

However,

"the maidens, if they have favorite swains, frequently decline playing for the pleasure of making love; for to all appearance it is the ladies, not the gentlemen, who nowadays show a preference. It is here, I fancy, always leap year . . . Lord!" Miss Franks closed her revelations, "if this letter is seen I shall be killed."

Some of it, too, was probably due to the excessive formality which enshrouded the movements of the first President. Always dignified, restrained, rather frigid—he was not a person to be slapped on the back, as Gouverneur Morris found out, at the expense of a wagered dinner and wine lost to Mr. Hamilton—George Washington during his presidency exhibited certain chilling austerities of deportment scarcely calculated to enliven that society which he graced with his presence. The matter was one of considerable concern to such ardent republicans as Mr. Jefferson, who professed to see in the aristocratic pomps and rituals of the "court" an immediate relapse into despotic monarchy. Nor were they soothed by the protracted efforts of some members of Con-

gress to hit upon a suitably highflown title for the
President. His High Mightiness, His Elective Majesty—these resounding appellations were solemnly
discussed, and while Mr. Washington disapproved of
them officially, one cannot but suspect that had they
met with more widespread support in influential leg-
islative circles he would have accepted them without
a qualm. The fact is that the stateliness of the recent
royal régime was strongly imprinted upon the minds
of many of the leading men of the early Federal era,
and that in ridding themselves of the Crown's authority it had not been their intention or expectation to
discard any of the distinctions and graces of social or
public life as they had hitherto experienced it. Independence did not, as they conceived it, involve any
diminution of ceremonial and address. The real
trouble was, they were a little self-conscious about it.

And one may not, presumably, speculate on the
effect which President Washington's personal state
of mind may have had upon his external bearing.
In 1758, he had wished that he were happy. Can
one be certain, in all respect and affection for Martha,
that in 1790, or at any time during his life, he was—
fundamentally, in his inmost, secret heart—any happier. . . .

But when all is said and done, if Martha was dis-
contented, if she was bored, if she was ill at ease, it
was, perhaps, primarily due to her own self. She was

a sweet, charitable, gracious little woman, enormously industrious and capable in the realm only of those domestic, simple, unpretentious pursuits which she understood and enjoyed. She had patience, fortitude and courage; she had a solid, almost massive, dignity, the ample poise of her rural gentility. But she was not a woman of the world—she was not Mrs. Jay or Mrs. John Adams—under her stiff brocades and her vast decorum she was apprehensive of her capacities; her very dignity lacked that sparkle of wit, that felicity of instinct, that lustre of manner for which, in those exacting diplomatic and political circles, it needed to be the setting. She was, in so many ways, a great lady; she can not be said to have been a *grande dame.*

"With respect to myself," she wrote, "I sometimes think the arrangement is not quite as it ought to have been, that I, who had much rather be at home, should occupy a place with which many younger and gayer women would be extremely pleased. . . . I am still determined to be cheerful and happy in whatever situation I may be."

She was, fortunately, greatly beloved and universally respected; and in the spring of 1790 there was a slight relaxation of severity. There were parties on the river and at Marriner's Tavern—which had once been the home of Mary Philipse Morris—and they attended the theatre a little. And in August they went to Philadelphia, using the state barge for the last time. And after they had gone, the gentlemen who had provided the barge proposed to present it to the Corporation, but the Corporation, who were feeling peevish at the removal of Government from New York, replied that "as this Board can have no use for the said barge, they decline the acceptance of her."

9

The question of the location of the national capital had finally been settled. It was to be Philadelphia for ten years, and after that Conogocheague on the Potomac, wherever that might be, a place—

"Where the houses and kitchens are yet to be framed,
The trees to be felled, and the streets to be named."

For months, Congress had done little else except argue this highly controversial point, while the Virginia, Pennsylvania and New York delegations scowled jealously at one another and enlisted the aid of intriguing lobbies. But now Mr. Morris, and Mr. Maclay, and the rest of them had won, and Philadelphia was delighted and New York disgruntled, but already the blessing was a little doubtful.

"Rents of houses," someone wrote from the Quaker City, "have risen and I fear will continue to rise

GEORGE WASHINGTON

From an engraving published in 1784 by Whitworth and Yates

shamefully . . . Whether the advantages we shall enjoy from the removal will be equivalent to the dis-
advantages time alone will determine. I am convinced, however, if things go on in this manner, a
very great majority of our citizens will have good reason to wish the government settled at Conogocheague
long before the ten years are expired."

And the Philadelphians had done a vast amount
of bragging about their precious city—they were a
self-complacent lot—but when the New Yorkers and
New Englanders, and the Virginians for that matter,
got there, there was nothing so very extraordinary
about it. "Philadelphia is a large and elegant city,"
Mr. Wolcott of Connecticut admitted, "but it did
not strike me with the astonishment which the citizens
predicted." And as for the people, all those famous
Chews, and Allens, and Penns, they were very proud
of their city, their wealth, and "their supposed knowledge," but "I have seen many of their principal men
and discover nothing that tempts me to idolatry. I
must see and examine before I say much, but I do
not expect that a more intimate acquaintance will fur-
nish me with any self-humiliating sensations."

Mr. Jeremiah Smith of New Hampshire thought
them, "from the highest to the lowest . . . a set of
beggars. You cannot turn around without paying a
dollar." And Mr. James Monroe declared flatly

that "the city seems at present to be mostly inhabited
by sharpers." Even the natives admitted it.

"You have never seen anything like the frenzy which
has seized upon the inhabitants here," a gentleman
wrote to a friend. "They have been mad ever since
the city became the seat of Government, and there
is no limit to their prodigality. . . . The probability
is that some families will find they cannot support
their dinners, suppers and losses at loo a great while;
but generally I believe the sharp citizens manage to
make temporary residents pay the bills, one way or
another."

In other respects, Philadelphia was not without
attractions.

"I have seen balls on the President's birthday," the
Duke de la Rochefoucauld-Liancourt observed,
"where the splendor of the rooms, and the variety and
richness of the dresses did not suffer in comparison
with Europe; and it must be acknowledged that the
beauty of the American ladies has the advantage in
the comparison. The young women of Philadelphia
are accomplished in different degrees, but beauty is
general with them. They want the ease and fashion
of Frenchwomen, but the brilliancy of their complexion is infinitely superior. Even when they grow old
they are still handsome; and it would be no exaggera-
tion to say in the numerous assemblies of Philadelphia it is impossible to meet with what is called a
plain woman. As for the young men," however,

"they for the most part seem to belong to another species."

Mr. Moreau de Saint Méry also thought the Philadelphia women beautiful, although he found them afflicted with bad teeth and nervous maladies. "American women are pretty," he said, "and the prettiest among them are those of Philadelphia. . . . This city presents them by the thousand from the ages of fourteen to eighteen." But in his opinion they soon lost their color, and if they were adorable at fifteen they were faded at twenty-three, old at thirty-five and decrepit at forty. And although they washed their faces and hands with great care, they never, he insisted, washed their mouths, seldom their feet, and even more rarely their bodies.

Maybe so; personal hygiene was subject to certain subterfuges in that day. But in spite of Mr. de Saint Méry—who had other fascinating observations to make concerning the young ladies of Philadelphia, whose freedom of social intercourse with the young men of their acquaintance never ceased to astonish and alarm him, almost as much as he was annoyed by their habit of "allowing gentlemen to pay for their purchases in the shops and then forgetting to reimburse them"—the fact remains that in Mrs. William Bingham, in the Misses Chew, in Miss Sally McKean, and in the Misses Allen, one of whom was considered the greatest beauty ever seen in America, Philadelphia could boast justifiably of as brilliant a native galaxy of belles as any other city could produce. And that in the competitive presence of the lovely Miss Wolcott, of Mrs. Otis, of Mrs. Ralph Izard, of Mrs. Elbridge Gerry, and of Mrs. John Jay, who had once, in a Paris theatre, been mistaken for Queen Marie Antoinette.

And all these ladies gave very splendid entertainments, which attained a degree of luxury which might have seemed unnecessarily extravagant, had they not been tempered by a simplicity and genuine cordiality of manners, to say nothing of an elegance and intellectual vivacity, which made Philadelphia society the envy of contemporary life. Mrs. Samuel Blodget, Mrs. John Adams, Mrs. William Bingham —when these great ladies of the world sat in state in their resplendent drawing rooms, there was gaiety spiced with an excellent wit, there was conversation enhanced by a ready culture, there was a most precise decorum graced by a matchless charm. A spirited scene, soon to be further enlivened, in 1794, by the winning exuberance of merry young Dolly Madison. And when the Chews, and the Clymers, and the McKeans gave parties, and at the Dancing Assemblies, the whole town came—that is to say the Third Street part of town—the girls in white brocaded silk trimmed with silver, with watches hanging from their tasselled sashes, and feathers in their hair; and Don Carlos de Yrujo, for one, who was soon to marry Sally McKean, all covered with gold lace and jewels.

But of them all, there was none more admired than Mrs. William Bingham—the Anne Willing whom the President had known as a child—the lady who had returned from a sojourn in Paris, London and The Hague to establish a *salon,* in her Third Street palace with the white marble staircase, which became a cherished legend in Philadelphia annals—and who died when she was not yet forty. . . .

10

And Martha had a much better time in Philadelphia than in New York. The Washingtons lived in one of Mr. Morris's houses on High Street; a double house possessing, according to Mr. Rush, an "external aspect marking it as the abode of opulence and respectability;" although Mr. Twining found it "a small red brick house . . . there was nothing in the exterior of the house that denoted the rank of its possessor. Next door was a hair dresser." A "neat but rather narrow staircase, carpeted in the middle," led upstairs and to "a middling sized well furnished drawing room on the left of the passage." The floor was carpeted, but "there were no pictures on the walls, no ornaments on the chimney piece." This was evidently not the room which contained the "medallions of Capet and his family," which so annoyed Citizen Minister Genêt when he viewed them.

Behind the house was a garden with trees; and beyond, on Minor Street, the stables in which were kept the family coach and two in which the President went to church—that noble, cream colored coach adorned with enamelled figures; and the carriage and four, for drives into the country; and Martha's own chariot and six—a London chariot, built originally for Governor John Penn, cream colored also, and embellished with richly gilded medallions. Something for Philadelphians to talk about, and for Mr. Jefferson to worry over, and for the white and scarlet liveried grooms to polish.

In that house on Christmas Day, 1790, the first levee was held and—

"you never could have seen such a drawing room," Sally McKean reported. "It was brilliant beyond anything you can imagine; and though there was a great deal of extravagance there was so much of Philadelphia taste in everything that it must have been confessed the most delightful occasion of the kind ever known in this country."

My eye and Betty Martin! In it, too, were given those quite pleasant, informal breakfasts and tea drinkings for which Martha herself filled the cups;

and those other tremendously ceremonious dinners, at which were served "an elegant variety of roast beef, veal, turkeys, ducks, fowls, hams, etc., puddings, jellies, oranges, apples, nuts, almonds, figs, raisins, and a variety of wines and punch"—and one may be sure that the latter were excellent, for the President ordered them himself from abroad, with discriminating fastidiousness.

And in Mr. Twining's upstairs room Martha held her own receptions, in a glow of chandeliers and lamps; those functions such as the one at which she sat—

"with Mrs. Knox near the fireplace; other ladies were seated on sofas, and gentlemen stood in the centre of the room conversing. On our approach Mrs. Washington arose and made a courtesy—the gentlemen bowed most profoundly—and I calculated my declension to her own with critical exactness."

Always a great deal of bowing in that house. . . .

Outside, in the town, they went to the play, occasionally, at the Southwark Theatre and the New, on Chestnut Street, or to Ricketts' Circus to see Mrs. Ricketts ride two horses at once, fearless woman; they did a great deal of visiting, in the city and at the country estates; and they attended the Birthday Balls; that tremendous one in 1795, where the seats were arranged in an amphitheatre and the dancing space roped off, and at which Miss Charlotte Chambers saw Martha seated next to—

"the wives of the foreign ambassadors, glittering from the floor to the summit of their head dress. One of the ladies wore three large ostrich feathers. Her brow was encircled by a sparkling fillet of diamonds; her neck and arms were almost covered with jewels, and *two* watches were suspended from her girdle. . . . Such superabundance of ornament struck me as injudicious."

And that last one in 1797, concerning which Miss Sally Cox announced that—

"it is to be the most superb entertainment I hear that ever has been here. . . . I suppose it will be a genteel mob. . . . Half Trenton is down already and I hear that *all* Princeton will be here. . . . I talk of taking two pairs of shoes with me."

11

The years passed. Very simply and quietly, really, when there was no company; for, whenever possible, Martha always retired early, with Nellie Custis in attendance to read a chapter from the Bible and sing a hymn for her. Very agreeably, in Martha's group of special friends—Mrs. Knox, Mrs. Morris, Mrs. Hamilton, Mrs. Bradford, Mrs. Powell. A group which did not, apparently, include Mrs. John Adams, whose husband was mortally jealous of the President.

In fact, the great Bingham, Blodget, Adams coterie cannot be said to have depended on the presence of the Washingtons for its brilliance.

Twice there was the yellow fever; quite seriously in 1793, but the President was so occupied that summer with Citizen Genêt's affairs that he stayed in town until September. And in 1794, again, they were too busy to go home, and took a house instead at Germantown for the hot weather. But other Congressional recesses found them at Mount Vernon, receiving delegations of Indians, whose visits—sometimes a dozen solemn chiefs at a time—finally took on the character of visitations; but in the midst of his manifold obligations the President never forgot that he was also the Great White Father of his country.

And then, on September 17, 1796, Mr. Washington issued his farewell address. A prudent document which was received with roars of scornful disapproval by the mass of Democratic Republicans in the country—those gentlemen who were anti-Federalists, who had stoned Mr. Hamilton at New York, who swore by Mr. Jefferson, supported the cause of revolutionary France and wore tri-colored cockades in their hats. The people Martha referred to as "filthy democrats," and accused of leaving dirty finger marks on her wall paper—for that good lady was not without a certain prejudicial acidity of temperament.

"George Washington!" they exclaimed—a man

who had hoped to make himself king of America; a proud, stuffy, conceited, ill-tempered, anglomaniac aristocrat; a man who had always conducted himself in office with the arrogance and ostentation of an "eastern pashaw," a despot, a tyrant, and, if Mr. Benjamin Franklin Bache was to be believed, a person of disreputable character, a cheat and an embezzler, in fact, a hyena and a crocodile.   So Mr. Jefferson's supporters maintained, and helped to embitter the closing years of the administration of that harassed, disgusted and pathetically tired gentleman on High Street whom Senator Maclay—on a page of his diary which ends abruptly in mid-sentence —described as—

"in stature about six feet with an unexceptional make, but lax appearance. His frame would seem to want filling up. His motions rather slow than lively. . . . His complexion pale, nay, almost cadaverous. His voice hollow and indistinct, owing as I believe to artificial teeth, before his upper jaw. . . ."

But a successor must now be found for him, and that it would be either Mr. Jefferson or Mr. John Adams soon became evident. The talk began again, in a whirlwind of handbills and pamphlets. George Washington had been bad enough, the Democratic Republicans insisted, but who was John Adams? "This man Adams!" A man who hated the French Revolution, a monarchist, an aristocrat; a man who talked about the "swinish multitudes," and the "well born" who should govern them; the husband of that Mistress Abigail who called the people of America the "mobility." To all of which the Federalists replied with prolonged guffaws of laughter at the expense of that gawk, that zany Mr. Jefferson. And who, in Heaven's name, was he? A man who invented whirligig chairs, who spent his time discoursing about fossils and philosophy, a scholar, a mere college professor. And aside from that, an atheist, a Jacobin, a demagogue, a coward who, in his political dealings, made use of the scurrilous pens of anonymous hirelings—and if Mr. Madison's ears burned at this he had only himself to blame.

So it went, while Mr. Thomas Paine was writing to the President that "as for you, Sir, treacherous in private friendship and a hypocrite in public life, the world will be puzzled to now decide whether you are an apostate or an impostor, whether you have abandoned good principles or whether you ever had any." But in February, 1797, Mr. Adams had been elected by three votes, and in March he was inaugurated. Mr. Washington was again a private citizen, and the *Aurora* graced the day by remarking that—

"when a retrospect is taken of the Washington administration for eight years, it is the subject of the greatest astonishment that a single individual should have cankered the principles of republicanism in an enlightened people just emerged from the gulf of despotism, and should have carried his designs against the public liberty so far as to have put in jeopardy its very existence. Such, however, are the facts, and with these staring us in the face this day ought to be a jubilee in the United States."

For Martha it very probably was. The Washingtons went home, and Nellie Custis said that "Grandpa is very well and much pleased with being once more Farmer Washington." It was the next year that he wrote to Sally Fairfax. . . .

12

It was nice to be home, after being a sort of "perambulator," as Martha expressed it. "I cannot tell you," she wrote to Mrs. Knox, "how much I enjoy home after been deprived of one so long. . . . The General and I feel like children just released from school or from a hard taskmaster. . . . We are so penurious with our enjoyment that we are loath to share it with anyone but dear friends. . . . I am again fairly settled down to the pleasant duties of an old fashioned Virginia housekeeper, steady as a clock, busy as a bee, and cheerful as a cricket." Perhaps in those few closing sentences Martha is appraised more closely than in all the inquisitive pages of more lengthy biographies. There is the real Martha as she was, as she would always have preferred to be, liberated from the restraints and rituals of a public life for which neither her tastes nor her talents had ever fitted her, however perfectly she might have achieved the semblance of ease in their fulfillment.

It was very pleasant at Mount Vernon, and she enjoyed herself. There were visits to make and receive—so *many* to receive; there were Philadelphia friendships to maintain; the house was always full, now, of Nellie Custis's beaux, and on February 22, 1799, "about candle light," she was married to Lawrence Lewis. It was very pleasant—and then, in December of that year, the General took cold. On the evening of December 14, he died. "'Tis well," Martha told them. "All is now over. I shall soon follow him. I have no more trials to pass through."

He was buried, first, in the lawn, and when Congress proposed that his remains be transferred to Washington City—for so Conogocheague was to be called—Martha replied that—

"taught by the great example which I have so long before me never to oppose my private wishes to the public will—I must consent to the request made by Congress . . . and in doing this I need not—I cannot say what a sacrifice of individual feeling I make to a sense of public duty."

The undertaking was, of course, abandoned, and for some two years Martha lived in the small attic room to which she had moved, busy with her knitting beside the little window which overlooked the green surface of his resting place.

Many visitors still came to see her; her adopted children were near her, and they brought to her other grandchildren and great-grandchildren; her countenance was "very little wrinkled and remarkably fair for a person of her years," she kept in touch with the world and, with all her old scorn of the "filthy democrats" who were now in power, "her remarks were frequently pointed, and sometimes very sarcastic, on the new order of things and the present administration."

She died on May 22, 1802, of the fever, after an illness of seventeen days. "To those amiable and Christian virtues which adorn the female character," the Washington *Federalist* recorded, "she added dignity of manners, superiority of understanding, a mind intelligent and elevated. The silence of respectful grief is our best eulogy."

And at Bath, in England, Sally Fairfax lived on for almost another decade, until she too died, in her eighty-first year. . . .

Abigail Adams

ABIGAIL ADAMS

1

DURING the first thirty years of the American Republic, it seemed as though all political roads led from Virginia, in whose red soil, according to Mr. John Randolph, Presidents grew; with one exception, when a Massachusetts Adams came out of New England to break the sequence of the Virginia dynasty, bringing with him his Puritan wife.

She was born at Weymouth, Massachusetts; Abigail, daughter of Elizabeth Quincy and Parson William Smith, a somewhat worldly prelate who paid fifteen pounds for his wigs, and prayed to the Lord "for S to res T," as he wrote it down in abbreviated sentences in his diary. On November 11, 1744—an unfortunate circumstance, since, at that time of the year in the frostbitten Colony, it was more than likely that they had to break the ice for her in the christening font. However, she was probably wrapped in a fine, new, handwoven "bearing cloth;" the midwife and the other women who had served her mother were treated to a good dinner, perhaps with "groaning beer;" and the first time she was moved, she was undoubtedly carried upstairs to insure her rise in the world, with gold and silver in her hands to bring her wealth, and scarlet on her head to keep her from harm. And not long afterwards they were hanging anodyne necklaces around her throat, and rubbing her gums with honey and butter mixed in with the boiled brains of a hare.

Perhaps the most extraordinary thing about her is that she should have survived the perils of her New England childhood, at a time when infants died almost as fast as they were born from a multitude of ailments, including "bladders in the windpipe;" and that she should not have succumbed, on the other hand, to the remedies which they forced into her reluctant system. She was a delicate child, and from Mrs. Earle's books on New England in Colonial days one may learn what happened to delicate children. She was, in the first place, certainly not allowed to remain in low spirits, for melancholy was an illness for which "applications" were given, in order to "drive the worms out of the brain as well as dross out of the stomack." If she had "collick"—which seems inevitable—they gave her ghastly concoctions of senna and rhubarb, mithridate with its forty-five ingredients, and Venice treacle, consisting, among a great many other substances, of opium, white wine and vipers. For rickets she would have imbibed quantities of Daffy's Elixir; and if she had fits or worms—many New England children did— there was nothing but "the admirable and famous Snail Water." And Snail Water was made as follows—and the recipe is not any more complicated or revolting than most—

"Take a peck of garden Shel Snails, wash them well in Small Beer, and put them in an oven till they have done making a Noise, then take them out and wipe them well from the green froth that is upon them, and bruise them shels and all in a Stone Mortar; then take a Quart of Earthworms, scoure them with salt"—how does one "scoure" an earthworm?— "slit them, and wash well with water from their filth, and in a stone Mortar beat them in pieces; then lay in the bottom of your distilled pot Angelica two handfuls, and two handfuls of Celandine upon them, to which put two quarts of Rosemary flowers, Bearsfoot, Agrimony, red Dock roots, Bark of Barberries, Betony wood, Sorrel of each two handfuls, Rue one handful; then lay the Snails and Worms on top of the hearbs and flowers, then pour on three Gallons of the strongest Ale and let it stand all night; in the morning put in three ounces of cloves beaten, sixpennyworth of beaten Saffron, and on top of them six ounces of shaved Hartshorne; then set on the Limbeck and close it with paste and so receive the water by pintes, which will be nine in all; the first is the strongest, whereof take in the morning two

spoonfuls in four spoonfuls of Small Beer, the like
in the afternoon."

Aside from that, she ate a great deal of corn, and
"askutasquash," and "sukquttahhash;" her full share
of "pumpion pye" with the caudle of white wine and
six "yelks of eggs;" and perhaps of "secret pye,"
which was potatoes boiled and blanched, seasoned
with spices and roots, covered with butter, sugar and
grape verjuice, and iced with rosewater. The secret
was the potatoes. A quantity, too, of apple slump
and crowdy, of marmalet and quiddonies, of rock
and Angelica candy, and of egg cakes and marche-
panes. And perhaps in her family they still thought
it best that young children should have their beer a
little heated, and take it with a piece of brown bread,
while their elders were consuming ale and cider, cal-
ibogus, rum-bullion, "bellows top" flip, black strap,
Salem "whistle-belly-vengeance," and metheglin,
which must be put into a vessel with a peg to give it
vent "when you hear it make a noise, which it will
do."

2

Abigail was spared the grim pedantry of New
England school rooms; she was always sick, and in
any case, "female education," she records, "in the
best families, went no further than writing and arith-

metic, in some few and rare instances, music and dancing"—and so she was never sent to any school. But her father was a man of parts; in her grandfather Quincy's home at Mount Wollaston there was a fine library; and at her grandmother's knee she received a more lasting education, perhaps, than would have been her lot elsewhere. One must not forget Grandmother Quincy, for it was she who, to a great extent, fashioned the intellect of the future first ambassadress to the Court of St. James.

One imagines Abigail learning her letters from old horn books and cardboard "battledores;" thumbing the pages of *The Child's New Spelling Book,* and picking her way through the virtuous paragraphs of the *New England Primer* and various "readamadeasies;" one sees her poring over copybooks in which she inscribed the intricacies of gothic, running secretary and round text penmanship; puzzling over sumbooks in which she put down the results of ascending and descending reduction, of the Rule of False and the Backer Rule of Thirds, and of the accumulations of anchors, tierces and kilderkins, of pottles, cooms, weys and lasts, as set forth in Mr. Wingate's—or was it Cocker's—"Arithmetick." And finding leisure to read Mr. John Newberry's imported books— *Nurse Truelove's book of books for children,* for instance, *adorned with cuts and designed as a present for . . . every little girl who would become a great woman and ride in a lord mayor's gilt coach*—to say nothing of—

"The Exact Account of the Conversion, Holy and Exemplary Lives and Joyful Deaths of Several Young Children, by James Janeway; to which is added a Token for the Children of New England, or some Examples of Children in whom the Fear of God was remarkably Budding before they died;"

a cheerful and enormously popular work, characteristic of the morbid piety of her day which compelled even little children to an enthusiastic, though frequently terrified, contemplation of the more gruesome aspects of the angel of death.

At the same time, she learned to spin, to weave, and to sew, to do frost work, and purles, and finny stitch; to paint on velvet, perhaps, and cut out flowers and escutcheons in "papyrotamia." And she learned to bake, and brew, and preserve, to make cordials and syrops—clove, gillyflower, borage, marjoram, poppy water, elecampane root, usquebarb and hypocras.

And when she had a moment to herself, she went out into the garden in her little wigs and stiff gowns, and played chuckie-stones with her friends; until she grew up, and then she began writing letters, many letters to "Myra," and "Aspasia," and "Aurelia," which she signed "Diana." But when she began writing letters to a certain young Mr. Adams, she signed those "Portia," for he was a lawyer.

3

And just because young John Adams, of Braintree, was a lawyer, he had a difficult time convincing Abigail's family—all but the Parson himself—that he was a suitable aspirant for her favor. He was a lawyer, which was to say, in contemporary estimation, that he was probably dishonest; and he was only descended, as he himself freely admitted, "from a line of virtuous, independent New England farmers." He was, also, "of an amorous disposition," and "fond of the society of females," although his "youthful flames were all modest and virtuous girls, and always maintained their character through life."

In other respects, he was presentable enough, even though he did resemble "a short, thick Archbishop of Canterbury;" he had graduated from Harvard College, in 1755, the year of the earthquake; he had taught school for a while at Worcester, in "a school of affliction" where he ran the risk of becoming "a base weed and ignoble shrub" from instructing "a large number of little runtlings just capable of lisping ABC;" and more recently he had taken up the practice of the law in Massachusetts, with very considerable success, sitting in the Council Chamber of the Town House at a long table with all the barristers at law of Boston "in gowns, bands and tiewigs," before the judges "all arrayed in their new, fresh, rich, robes of scarlet English broadcloth, in their large cambric bands and immense judicial wigs."

And in 1764 he was courting Abigail, making love to her, perhaps, through a primitively telephonic "courting stick," in the presence of her elders; and she was sending him "love, respects, good wishes, regards—a whole waggon load of them," and writing to him every day, and wondering whether she would not—

"make my letters very cheap? Don't you light your pipe with them? I care not if you do. 'Tis a pleasure to me to write. Yet I wonder I write to you with so little restraint, for as a critic I fear you more than any other person on earth, and 'tis the only character in which I ever did or ever will fear you."

And so, with Parson Smith to back them up, they were married, on October 25, 1764. And for his wedding text Parson Smith took "For John came neither eating bread nor drinking wine, and ye say he hath a devil," which was one on the family; and one may be sure that Abigail likewise chose a spirited one for her "coming out" Sunday.

During the next ten years—while the children were being born, little Abigail, Johnny Quincy, Charles and Thomas—they lived in Braintree, and in Boston; in a white house on Brattle Square, in Mrs. Fayer-

weather's house on Cole Lane, in another house on
Brattle Square, in one on Queen Street—until John
wrote that "I hope I shall not have occasion to remove
so often." And almost at once there were tribulations.

The Stamp Act, in 1765, when the courts were
closed by the Governor, so that it seemed to John
that the Bar were behaving—

"like a flock of shot pigeons," and that "so sudden an
interruption in my career is very unfortunate for me.
I was but just getting into my gears, just getting under sail, and an embargo is laid upon the ship." He
had "but just become known and gained a small degree of reputation when this execrable project was
set on foot for my ruin as well as that of America in
general and of Great Britain."

But just when the prospect was dreariest, he was appointed to represent the town of Boston before the
Governor for the purpose of requesting the reopening
of the courts.

And again, in 1770, when some hoodlums made
merry with a British sentry on King Street, so that
Captain Preston and a dozen men came bundling out
and killed five citizens of Boston before the riot could
be quieted. For the next day Captain Preston implored John Adams to defend him, since he could
get no one else to accept his case, and John saw him-

self obliged to chose between his personal popularity —and it might be the safety of his family and his own—and what he conceived to be his plain duty as a lawyer. But Abigail, "that excellent lady who has always encouraged me," although she burst into a flood of tears and expressed her dread of the danger to themselves and to their children, told him that he was right; and so he took the case, which brought him exactly eighteen guineas, and secured the acquittal of the Captain and his clumsy grenadiers. But after all nothing happened, and John was elected to be one of the representatives of Boston in Town Meeting, in spite of the trial.

And then, in 1773, there was real trouble brewing, even though at first it was only a question of how tea should be "brewed." As the famous song said—

"There was an old lady lived over the sea,
And she was an Island Queen.
Her daughter lived off in a new countrie,
With an ocean of water between.
The old lady's pockets were full of gold,
But never contented was she;
So she called on her daughter to pay her a tax
Of three pence a pound on her tea."

But Boston did not propose to pay any tax, fond as she was of Hyson and Bohea.

"Now Mother, dear Mother, the daughter replied,
I shan't do the thing you ax.

I'm willing to pay a fair price for the tea,
But never the three penny tax.
You shall, quoth the mother, and reddened with rage,
For you're my own daughter, you see,
And sure 'tis quite proper the daughter should pay
Her mother a tax on her tea."

And still Boston did not propose to pay any tax.
Rather let the "weed of slavery" be tossed overboard
—and it was an open secret that the "Mohawks" were
preparing to raid the tea ship. For while Abigail's
heart beat a little faster at every whistle in the street,
John was writing in his diary that "twenty-eight
chests of tea arrived yesterday, which are to make an
infusion in water at seven o'clock this evening." And
so—

"The tea was conveyed to the daughter's door,
All down by the ocean side,
And the bouncing girl poured out every pound
In the dark and boiling tide.
And then she called out to the Island Queen,
Oh, Mother, dear Mother, quoth she,
Your tea you may have when 'tis steeped enough
But never a tax from me."

But in June, 1774, things had gone too far, and John
Adams was appointed a member of the Massachusetts Committee to the Congress at Philadelphia.
"The die is now cast," he said. "To swim or sink,
live or die, survive or perish with my country is my

unalterable determination." He moved his family to Braintree, and on August 10 he set forth for Philadelphia.

"We live, my dear soul, in an age of trial," he told Abigail. "What will be the consequence I know not. . . . "

4

For Abigail there was to be only one consequence. The whole Revolution, the coming of the minute men to take her pewter spoons, Bunker Hill, the guns booming over Boston, the constant peril of her situation, sickness, anxiety, financial care—these could all be borne, with that fortitude which was her new England heritage, that resignation which was her Puritan dowry. The one consequence that mattered, the one circumstance which was unbearable, and still must be borne, was that from that day in August, 1774, with the exception of a few scattered months, she was separated for ten years—once for a whole solid four—from her beloved husband.

There are many inspiring aspects of Abigail Adams during this period. Abigail caring for the four children, nursing them through illnesses, she who was herself so much an invalid, taking them to be inoculated for the smallpox—though probably not by "Isbrahim Mustapha, Inoculator to his Sublime Highness and Janissaries" and more lately of Boston, giving lessons

to Charles and Thomas, and improving the hours, no
doubt, with *Mr. Winlove's Collection of Moral Tales;*
chivying Johnny Quincy out of her closet, where, in
a haze of precocious tobacco smoke, he was in vain
endeavoring to discover the "recondite charm" of Mr.
Milton's *Paradise Lost;* teaching "Nabby" to sew and
spin, and perhaps help make "bounty coats" for the
soldiers, seeing that she did her duty by *The Young
Lady's Accidence,* and supervising the samplers on
which, like little Mary Jackson, she may have embroidered her conviction that—

> "Abigail Adams is my name,
> America my nation,
> Boston is my dwelling place,
> And Christ is my salvation."

Abigail doing everything in her power to obey her
husband's request that she train her children to virtue, "habituate them to industry, activity and spirit;
make them consider every vice as shameful and un-
manly; fire them with ambition to be useful;" and
that she see to it that every decency, grace and honesty be inculcated upon them. "For God's sake,
make your children hardy, active and industrious!"

Abigail at Braintree, making every article of cloth-
ing, all the linen, all the blankets, for the household;
manufacturing soap and other domestic necessities;
attending to the farm, to the dairy, to the "husbandry," and saving the precious pennies; for—

"I must entreat you," John wrote, "my dear partner in all the joys and sorrows, prosperity and adversity of my life, to take a part with me in the struggle. I pray God for your health—entreat you to rouse your whole attention to the family, the stock, the farm, the dairy. Let every article of expense which can possibly be spared be retrenched. . . . My life has been a continual scene of fatigue, vexation, labor and anxiety. I have four children. I had a pretty estate from my father; I have been assisted by your father; I have done the greatest business in the province; I have had the very richest clients in the province; yet I am poor, in comparison with others."

Abigail in the midst of war's very close alarms—so that she must be sure, "in case of real danger," to "fly to the woods with our children"—so bewildered in anticipation, so calm and sane in emergency—so that John could write to her of the pleasure it gave him—

"to learn that you sustain with so much fortitude the shocks and terrors of the times. You are really brave, my dear. You are a heroine and you have reason to be. . . . A soul as pure, as benevolent, as virtuous and pious as yours has nothing to fear . . . from the last of human evils."

Abigail the patriot, deeply concerned in the portentous affairs of the nation, writing so thoughtfully, so intelligently, on every topic, suggesting statecraft, telling her husband that women should have a share in government, and earning his praise for shining "as a stateswoman of late, as well as a farmeress." Abigail, serene and patient, while matters dragged so tediously at Philadelphia—"slow as snails"—where every man was "a great man, an orator, a critic, a statesman," and so "must show his oratory, his criticism and his political abilities" on every question, until petulant John Adams cried out in desperation—

"Posterity! You will never know how much it cost the present generation to preserve your freedom! I hope you will make good use of it. If you do not, I shall repent it in heaven that I ever took half the pains to preserve it!"

In all these respects, Abigail Adams was magnificent. She was the living spirit of the embattled Colonies, she was, essentially, New England—its bigotry inspired to tenacity, its harshness quickened into determination, its austerity illuminated by a fine resolve, its long tradition of sturdy faith and devotion—to the home, to the land and to God—strengthened and sweetened in the keeping of this gentle, loyal, courageous lady.

But in none of these aspects is she so appealing, so genuine, so sympathetic, as in her revelation as the wife of John Adams, who fretted and spent "many melancholy hours" over their continued separation; the woman "with so much sensibility," who longed

for her husband's return and could not be comforted
for his absence. A revelation which shines through
the pages of her tender, affectionate letters to him,
in which, because her pen was "always freer than my
tongue," she wrote "many things to you that I suppose I never could have talked." That five weeks
had passed and not one line from him, and "I would
rather give a dollar for a letter by the post, though
the consequence should be that I ate but one meal a
day these three weeks to come;" that every line he
sent her was "like a precious relic from the saints;"
and that she "dare not express to you . . . how ar-
dently I long for your return. I have some very miser-
ly wishes, and cannot consent to your spending one
hour in town, till, at least, I have had you twelve."

And finally John himself, in his stiff, undemon-
strative way, wrote to her from Philadelphia that
"I will never come here again without you, if I can
persuade you to come with me. Whom God has
joined together ought not to be put asunder so long,
with their own consent."

5

But the days of separation were not ended; they
were really just beginning. For in November, 1777,
Mr. Adams was chosen to go to France to help Mr.
Franklin, and in February, 1778, he sailed, taking
with him little eleven year old John Quincy. "How

ABIGAIL ADAMS

From the painting by Stuart

lonely are my days! How solitary my nights," poor
Abigail wrote. "Can the best of friends recollect
that for fourteen years past I have not spent a whole
winter alone?" And once, six months went by without
a word from him, and Abigail herself was obliged
to wait five before she could find a vessel to carry her
mail. And so many ships were captured, and the
precious letters lost. And Abigail could not stand
it; and she poured out her heart to him, and complained a little because he did not write more frequently and at greater length, and talked to him on
the written page as though he had been there with
her, telling him many tender, foolish things. And
John Adams was offended, and embarrassed, and told
her so, with that lack of patience and tact which so
distinguished him.

"For God's sake," he wrote in February, 1779,
"never reproach me again with not writing or with
writing scrips. Your wounds are too deep. You
know not, you feel not, the dangers that surround me.
. . . Millions would not tempt me to write you as I
used. I have no security that every letter I write
you will not be broken open, and copied, and trans-
mitted to Congress and to English newspapers . . . .
There are spies upon every word I utter and every
syllable I write. . . . My life has been often in danger, but I never considered my reputation and character so much in danger as now. I can pass for a fool,

but I will not pass for a dishonest or mercenary man. Be upon your guard therefore. I must be upon mine, and I will. . . . You complain that I don't write often enough, and that when I do my letters are too short. If I were to tell you all the tenderness of my heart, I should do nothing but write to you. . . . Let me entreat you to consider, if some of your letters had by any accident been taken, what a figure would they have made in a newspaper, to be read by the whole world? Some of them . . . would have done honor to the most virtuous and most accomplished Roman matron, but others of them would have made you and me very ridiculous."

Poor Abigail. For herself, she would not have cared at all. . . .

But there seemed to be nothing for Mr. Adams to do in Europe, "the dullest place in the world"— Congress forgot to send him any instructions—and in August, 1779, he was home once more. This time, surely, it was for good. No. In November of that year, Mr. Adams was ordered to France again, and the longest separation of all was at hand. And as the long years passed, 1780, 1781, 1782, Abigail wanted to go to France, but Mr. Adams did not think that life in Europe would be good for the children.

But when peace was signed, in 1783, and still Mr. Adams did not come home—but was sent to London, and to Holland, and spoken of as Minister to England—the matter was discussed again.

"I had much to do to persuade myself to venture a summer passage," Abigail assured her husband, "but a winter one I never could think of encountering. I am too much of a coward." And she did not want to go to England; she would have enjoyed visiting France for a year, "but to think of going to England in a public character, and engaging at my time of life in scenes quite new, attended with dissipation, parade and nonsense—I am sure I should make an awkward figure." No, her most ardent wish was to have him return—"my health is infirm . . . neither of us appears to be built for duration. Would to Heaven, the few remaining days allotted us might be enjoyed together!"

But in June, 1784, she sailed, with "Nabby"—who was not sorry, perhaps, to put away her copy of *The Amours and Adventures of Two English Gentlemen in Italy,* and see their prototypes in their native England.

6

It was a rough crossing, and they were all extremely seasick, since "the decency and decorum of the most delicate female must in some measure yield to the necessities of nature." And the little staterooms opening onto the cabin where the gentlemen slept were very crowded and confined; but fortunately it was a set of "well behaved, decent gentlemen, whose whole deportment is agreeable to the strictest delicacy, both in word and action." And then they were

at Osborn's Adelphi Family Hotel, in London, with
two rooms and three servants for three guineas a week
without food; and scores of Americans, many of them
expatriated Loyalists, were coming to call, and taking them to dinners where there were only two kinds
of meat on the table, although "invited several days
in advance;" and finally, in August, Mr. Adams arrived from Holland, preceded by John Quincy whom
his mother hardly recognized.

They left almost immediately for Paris, and soon
they were established in a spacious house at Auteuil,
in the suburbs, in which forty beds could be made, but
"with an expense of thirty thousand *livres* in looking
glasses, there is no table in the house better than an
oak board, nor a carpet belonging to the house." And
there were horrid tile floors everywhere, and a special
servant to polish them.   Abigail was very busy, ac-
customing herself to the domestics, selecting household goods, purchasing clothes in which to attend
dinners, and the theatre, and the opera.   For in Paris
Puritan New England must do as the Parisians, or
become utterly recluse.   But Paris was not much.

"They tell me I am no judge for that I have not seen
it yet. One thing I know, and that is that I have smelt
it. . . . It is the very dirtiest place I ever saw. . . .
Boston cannot boast so elegant public buildings, but
in other respects it is as much superior in my eyes to
Paris as London is to Boston."

As for the opera—

"the dresses and beauty of the performers were enchanting; but no sooner did the dance commence than I felt my delicacy wounded and I was ashamed to be seen to look at them. Girls clothed in the thinnest silk and gauze, with their petticoats short, springing two feet from the floor, poising themselves in the air, with their feet flying, and as perfectly showing their garters and drawers as though no petticoat had been worn, was a sight altogether new to me." La, Mrs. Adams! However, "shall I speak a truth, and say that repeatedly seeing these dances has worn off that disgust . . . and that I see them now with pleasure?" To be sure, "as soon as a girl sets her foot upon the floor of the opera she is excommunicated by the Church, and denied burial in holy ground."

And then, in May, 1785, the event that Abigail had dreaded took place; Mr. Adams was appointed Minister Plenipotentiary to England, and she found herself obliged to undertake the endlessly difficult rôle of America's first official ambassadress to the British capital, where she expected "to be more scrutinised" than in Paris. They went to London, and settled first at the Bath Hotel, Westminster, and later in a house on Grosvenor Square, and in June—while the Tory papers were pouring out their "venom" at this reception of the envoy from the revolted Colonies —they were presented at court; Abigail in an elegant but decently plain gown, "white lutestring, covered and full trimmed with white crape, festooned with lilac ribbon and mock point lace, over a hoop of enormous extent; there is only a narrow train of about three yards in length to the gown waist. . . . Ruffle cuffs for married ladies, treble lace, ruffles, a very dress cap with long lace lappets, two white plumes and a blonde lace handkerchief. This is my rigging. I should have mentioned two pearl pins in my hair, ear rings and necklace of the same kind."

"I would gladly be excused the ceremony," she wrote on the day of the function, but it all passed pleasantly enough, except for the four hours they were kept standing in the drawing room, and in spite of the somewhat artificial cordiality necessarily attendant upon an event so reminiscent of recent British disasters. The King was a personable man, although he had a red face and white eyebrows; the Queen was in purple and silver, and she was not well shaped, nor handsome. In fact, the ladies of the court in general were "very plain, ill shaped and ugly; but don't you tell anybody that I say so!"

As for the royal drawing rooms—

"I know I am looked down upon with a sovereign pride." But "I consider myself as complimenting the power before which I appear as much as I am complimented by being noticed by it. . . . Consequently I never expect to be a court favorite. Nor would I

ever again set my foot there if the etiquette of my
country did not require it."

It was all very trying and immensely difficult; the
scorn of the royal circle, the constant downpour of
scurrilous invective in the papers.

"Some years hence it may be a pleasure to reside here
in the character of American Minister; but with the
present salary and the present temper of the English,
no one need envy the embassy. There would soon be
fine work if any notice was taken of their billingsgate and abuse. . . . How would they exult, if they
could lay hold of any circumstance in either of our
characters to make us appear ridiculous."

How careful she had to be, how tactful, how gracious, how dignified, how unfailingly watchful. That
they never were made to appear ridiculous, must have
been due, in a large measure, to her own intelligence
and good sense, to her breeding, and to her faultless
instinct. This Puritan lady who was so afraid of appearing awkward. She had done many admirable
things in the past, she was to occupy a more exalted
station in her own land, but she was perhaps never
to conduct herself more admirably and with greater
courage than during the three perilously conspicuous
years of her embassy. And they had a good time with
it all. "Nabby" was married to Mr. Smith, of the
Legation, and the daughter of Abigail Smith Adams

became Abigail Adams Smith. And England was England, in spite of the Tory press—the River, Devonshire, Cornwall—and London was very gay. "But such a set of gamblers as the ladies here are. And such a life as they lead. . . . I will come and shelter myself in America from this scene of dissipation!"

And finally, in 1788, they went home, and there was to be rest, at last, and a little quiet "husbandry" at Braintree which Mr. Adams had not seen for nearly nine years. . . .

7

But America had not done yet with John Adams. He must be her first Vice President, and so, in 1789, Abigail had to come to New York, to the lovely mansion at Richmond Hill, beyond Lispenard's Meadows, in the pleasant village of Greenwich. A fine, porticoed mansion, surrounded by beautiful trees, in front of which "the noble Hudson rolls his majestic waves, bearing upon his bosom innumerable small vessels which are constantly forwarding the rich products of the neighboring soil to the busy hand of a more extensive commerce"—or so it seemed to Abigail's more maturely stately pen.

And soon, in 1790, she had to move to Philadelphia which was become the temporary seat of Government. To Bush Hill, where the sheep were pastured daily upon her lawn. "Bush Hill, as it is called, though by the way there remains neither bush nor shrub upon it . . . yet Bush Hill is a very beautiful place. But the grand and sublime I left at Richmond Hill!" The new house was better furnished, but the other had been more convenient in store rooms and closets. The rooms at Bush Hill were cold and damp, and nothing had been unpacked when they arrived, and still there were crowds of visitors to be received every day, from eleven in the morning until three. But they were better off than Mrs. Washington, whose house was not even finished.

And Philadelphia was very gay; the profusion and luxury at the tables of the wealthy, in their equipages, and the dresses of their wives and daughters were, as the Duke de la Rochefoucauld-Liancourt was moved to observe, extreme; there was a continuous round of routs, and tea, and cards—so that Abigail foresaw a very dissipated winter if she were to accept all the invitations which she received; there was the theatre where she witnessed *The School for Scandal;* there were great dinners and balls, graced by the presence of "the dazzling Mrs. Bingham and her beautiful sisters; the Misses Allen and the Misses Chew; in short a constellation of beauties." There were Assemblies where the dancing was very good and the company of the best, "but the room despicable, the etiquette—it was difficult to say where it was

found. Indeed, it was not New York; but you must
not report this from me!"

In fact, concerning Philadelphia as a whole, in the
Second Lady's sharply critical estimation, "when all
is said and done, it will not be Broadway!"

But Bush Hill was removed from the city, the
winter roads were all clay up to the horses' knees,
it was difficult to get around. And Abigail was not
well; she had just undergone a severe illness, and life
was a constant misery of recurring ailments. More
and more, during the second vice presidency and
after, she abandoned the wearisome gaieties of the
capital and sought refuge in the country. So that
after twenty years John and Abigail found themselves in the same dreary predicament—he fast at
his duties in Philadelphia for a good part of the year,
she in seclusion at Braintree, or Quincy as they now
called it.

8

It was all a great mistake, actually. Mr. Adams
was not qualified, temperamentally, to hold so public
an office, to preside over a body such as the Senate, in a position requiring the coolest dignity, the
most calculating tact. Vain, irritable, jealous, obstinate, fault finding—defects which had increased
with the years—he did not, at the same time, any
longer avoid being ridiculous. He had "neither

judgment, firmness of mind, nor respectability of deportment to fill the chair of such an assemblage." In his most pompous moments he allowed "an unmeaning kind of vacant laugh" to escape him, his face was dimpled by a foolish "simper." He permitted himself to criticize members from the chair; he was forever making fatuous speeches; he wasted the Senate's time by discussing whether a letter incorrectly addressed to him as "His Excellency" could be read by him, whether members should be styled Honorable or Right Honorable in the minutes, whether he should sign bills as Vice President or as President of the Senate. These matters, he felt, were "most important," and the Senate must remember that "Vice President is my title."

He was almost fanatic on this subject of titles. "You are against titles," he told Senator Maclay, "but there are no people in the world so much in favor of titles as the people of America, and the Government never will be properly administered until they are adopted in the fullest manner." He was a New Englander, and, as the Senator observed, "no people in the Union dwell more on trivial distinctions and matters of mere form. They really seem to show a readiness to stand on punctilio and ceremony." Mr. Adams did so to a degree which brought forth against him the accusation of being a monarchist, a lover of kings and nobility. He did so in the most childish ways—"When the President comes into the Senate," he solemnly asked that body, "what shall I be?" He was President of the Senate, but when Mr. Washington made one of his majestic entrances, "I cannot be president then. No, gentlemen, I cannot, I cannot. I wish gentlemen to think what I shall be." Gentlemen thought, with their tongues in their cheeks, and Mr. Izard finally decided, in private, that he should be "His Rotundity."

This was all extremely unfortunate, and Abigail would undoubtedly have taken him home if she had known some of the things that were being written and thought about him. How he was "full of small attentions," and so well qualified "to adjust the etiquette of loops and buttons" that he should have been a tailor. How the very principles which had actuated Dr. Rush and Senator Maclay, "when we puffed John Adams in the papers and brought him forward for Vice President," would probably also make him President. How he had been touted by them for the office merely because "we knew his vanity, and hoped by laying hold of it to render him useful among the New England men in our scheme of bringing Congress to Pennsylvania," and away from New York.

But there, at least, they found him "the most unmanageable of all brutes," because "his pride, obstinacy and folly" were equal to his vanity—and, a thing which the Senator forgot to mention, because ethically he was above reproach. And, as they foresaw it, when Mr. Washington retired in 1796, Mr. Adams was his obvious successor. Old John Adams, the patriot, the public servant. The Republicans might rail at his ambitious monarchism, his egotism, his follies, and set up against him that paragon of democratic virtues, Mr. Thomas Jefferson, inventor of whirligig chairs—the Federalists had not yet done with Government, and Mr. Adams was elected, if only by three votes.

"My feelings are not those of pride or ostentation upon the occasion," Abigail wrote to him on his inauguration day in 1797. "They are solemnised by a sense of the obligations, the important trusts, and numerous duties connected with it. That you may be enabled to discharge them with honor to yourself, with justice and impartiality to your country, and with satisfaction to this great people, shall be the daily prayer of your A. A."

She was suffering then from "the depradations of time," from indispositions which hastened its strides and impaired "a frail fabric;" she had felt very keenly too, the party abuse of the campaign; she would have done well—she who was so good a judge of men, who made "some pretensions to physiognomy," who knew her husband so much better than he knew himself—to have taken him by the hand and led him quietly back to Quincy.

9

For in his presidency Mr. Adams was not to be any more fortunate, any more dignified though infinitely pompous, any more amenable to reason and common sense. He witnessed the last flareup of Federalist popularity—the days of the French war and the Black Cockade parades in his honor; the days of the *President's March* and *Hail Columbia* in the theatres; the days of the *New Yankee Doodle,* and—

> "Our sheet anchor's sure,
> And our bark rides secure,
> So here's to the toast
> We Columbians boast,
> The Federal Constitution
> And the President for ever!"

But he antagonized his party and disrupted it into "Adamites" and "Pickeronians;" he quarreled stupidly with his secretaries, and drove two of them out of his Cabinet, accusing them of conspiracy against him with Mr. Hamilton; he finally saw himself viciously attacked by the latter—in a pamphlet "concerning the public conduct and character of John Adams" which Mr. Hamilton, that busy destroyer of reputations, had prepared for private circulation, but of which a copy was stolen from the printer and taken to Colonel Burr, so that he might issue extracts

from it to a delighted Republican world.   Before
long everyone was singing—

> "See Johnny at the helm of State,
>   Head itching for a crowny;
> He longs to be, like Georgy, great,
>   And pull Tom Jeffer downy!"

But Mr. Hamilton was not altogether wrong in his
estimate of Mr. Adams.

"Of a restless and irritable temperament"—it is Mr.
George Gibbs summing up more dispassionately—
—"jealous of others' praise and suspicious of their
influence; obstinate and yet fickle . . . and vain to
a degree approaching insanity; he was himself in-
capable alike of conceiving or of acting upon a settled
system of policy, and was to others as easy a subject for indirect management as he was imprac-
ticable to more legitimate approach. . . . When, in
addition to errors of judgment, faults of the heart
also are disclosed; when the magistrate yields himself
to suspicion and envy, to the indulgence of personal
animosity and the gratification of a vanity which re-
fuses counsel and is obstinate in wrong . . . our sorrow gives way to indignation. . . . The presidential
career of Mr. Adams furnishes a pitiable instance of
how completely the mistakes, and still more the faults
of maturer years blot out the remembrance of early
and important services."

Mr. Adams was not utterly unaware of it himself.

"It is an awful reflection," he wrote to his daughter in 1796, "that every weakness, every folly, every resentful, vindictive, malignant passion of the heart, which in the vigor of understanding may be corrected or suppressed, must break out and show itself to the world and posterity from the trembling lips and shaking hands of seventy or eighty years. May my farm and family only be witnesses of my dotages when they must arrive."

But his "dotages" came upon him, and he was still in public office. Perhaps if Abigail had been more constantly at his side she could have avoided them for him, restrained his angers as she occasionally censored his correspondence, guided him into less arrogant ways. Unless it were that she, too, had grown more intolerant with the passing years, more scornful of the "mobility," less clear sighted in her understanding of him. As it was, she painstakingly discharged such social duties as her health would permit; she held her levees which were a little more sprightly than those of Mrs. Washington; she moved majestically through the great drawing rooms of the day, Mrs. Izard's, Mrs. Jay's, Mrs. Gerry's, Mrs. Blodget's; she went, sometimes, to Mrs. Bingham's famous balls, where they began to serve the punch immediately after the first dance, and "the best as well as the prettiest" ice cream was carried around in splendid china cups with gold spoons, and the supper table

His Excellency JOHN ADAMS.

JOHN ADAMS

From an engraving published in 1783 by J. Fielding

was decorated with real orange trees, and "you can't
think how beautiful it looked"—at least, to Mrs.
Benjamin Stoddert.

10

And then, in November, 1800, they made her move
to Washington City, since the Government was now
to be there—and as Richmond Hill had been superior to Bush Hill, so Bush Hill was immeasurably
preferable to Washington. In fact, Washington, as
a city, was practically non-existent. One wing only
of the Capitol had been erected, which, with the President's white sandstone House, was a striking object
"in dismal contrast" with the surrounding scene.
Not an avenue or street was visible, except the New
Jersey avenue—a mere road with two buildings on
it—and the Pennsylvania, which for considerable
stretches ran through a deep morass covered with
alder bushes. Its recognizable portions were lined
with double rows of Lombardy poplars guarding a
pathway usually filled with stagnant water; in dry
weather the avenue was all dust, in wet weather all
mud, and along it "the Royal George, an old fashioned"—old fashioned in 1800—"long bodied, four
horse stage, either rattled with members of Congress
from Georgetown in a halo of dust, or pitched like
a ship in a seaway among the holes and ruts of this
national highway."

There were buildings enough in the city to accommodate Congress, Abigail found, if they had been compact and finished, "but as they are, and scattered as they are, I see no great comfort for them." They must lodge, otherwise, at Mr. Peacock's on the Jersey Avenue, or at Blodget's Great Hotel, or at Tunnecliffe's on Capitol Hill, or at the Union Tavern in Georgetown, where Mr. Adams first found shelter. As for the President's House, it was on a grand and superb scale, requiring about thirty servants, and so well proportioned, consequently, to the President's salary! The lighting of it, alone, was a "tax indeed," and the fires "we are obliged to keep to secure us from daily agues is another very cheerful comfort." And to assist them——

"in this great castle . . . bells are wholly wanting, not one single one being hung in the whole house. . . . If they will put me up some bells, and let me have wood enough to keep fires, I design to be pleased . . . but surrounded with forests, can you believe that wood is not to be had, because people cannot be found to cut and cart it."

The house was habitable, but aside from that there was not a single apartment finished, they had "not the least fence, yard, or other convenience without; and the great unfinished audience room I make a drying room of, to hang up the clothes in." The principal stairs were not up, and would not be that winter; only six chambers were comfortable, two for the President, two lower rooms, one for a parlor and one for levees. And because the ladies of Washington seemed to expect it, Abigail turned to and held one, in the oval drawing room where they had put the crimson furniture.

This was Abigail Adams at her cheerful, philosophical, loyal best again—that elderly, invalid lady of fifty-six. And it was not as though she had been expecting to stay in Washington; there had just been a presidential campaign, in which "the instruments made use of and the means which were practised to effect a change" had her "utter abhorrance and detestation, for they were the blackest calumny and the foulest falsehoods;" and the consequence was "that we retire from public life."

"For myself and family," she wrote, "I have few regrets. At my age, and with my bodily infirmities, I shall be happier at Quincy. Neither my habits, nor my education or inclination, have led me to an expensive style of living, so that on that score I have little to mourn over. If I did not rise with dignity I can at least fall with ease. . . I feel not any resentment against those who are coming into power . . . I leave to time the unfolding of a drama. I leave to posterity to reflect upon the times past, and I leave them characters to contemplate."

Mr. Jefferson, Colonel Burr, the whole retinue of Republicanism. Perhaps one of her finest and truest letters. Whatever Mr. Adams may have done, there was nothing ridiculous, nothing petty, nothing ignoble about Abigail Adams. She left Washington in the spring, and during the early hours of March 4, 1801, Mr. Adams rolled peevishly out in his coach on the road to Massachusetts, after signing a great many Federal appointments for the "midnight judges." And as he rattled through Baltimore and Philadelphia, he saw the flares of bonfires, he heard the booming of guns and the pealing of bells, he witnessed the processions, the civic and military parades, the red liberty caps on the poles, with which a jubilant nation was greeting the inauguration of the Mammoth of Democracy, the downfall of "Bonny Johnny," and the passing of an aristocratic era. . . .

11

And now at last they were back at Quincy, in old Braintree, for good. In a fine mansion, built by Leonard Vassall, set in the midst of spreading, elm shaded lawns. Abigail's health did not improve, but still that energetic woman was getting up at five o'clock in summer to perform the "operations of dairywoman," and in winter kindling her own fire at six, and stirring all over the house to arouse its inmates to their manifold domestic duties. And still

writing innumerable letters, sometimes until eleven
o'clock at night.

And if she had retired, and gladly, from public
life, Abigail had not forgotten the circumstances
which had brought about that retirement, she had not
become reconciled to the "blackest calumny and the
foulest falsehoods" which had so offended her husband and embittered his recollection of the years
spent in the country's service, and she had not for-
given those whom she considered responsible for the
affronts to which he had been subjected—the vicious
attacks upon his character, the apparent treachery
of former associates, the deliberate hostility of dis-
loyal friends.

And so, in 1804, she wrote to Mr. Jefferson, who
had once been a good friend and was now one no
longer. It was simply a letter of condolence, written
on the occasion of the death of Mr. Jefferson's daughter, Polly Eppes, whom Abigail had known and cared
for as a little girl in London. A letter written in
kindness and sympathy, for old times' sake, to a bereaved father, but not in friendship for the man, not
with any intent to bridge the gulf which must inevitably remain between her husband's enemy and herself. A sincere letter, genuine in sentiment, generously conceived, but utterly uncompromising in spirit.
A courteous, seemly letter without a trace of cordiality or conciliation. But Mr. Jefferson replied to it,

stating his own grievance against Mr. Adams; and from these beginnings there developed a spirited interchange of letters between her husband's successor and Abigail, conducted entirely without the knowledge of Mr. Adams—although he was eventually made aware of it by her—in which the incidents which had estranged the two men were openly discussed, and the way undoubtedly paved for the reconciliation which finally reunited these two old friends.

There was, Mr. Jefferson had written, only one act of Mr. Adams's life which had ever given him "a moment's personal displeasure," and that was when Mr. Adams had made his last appointments to office, just before retiring from the presidency. Mr. Jefferson considered them as "personally unkind; they were from my most ardent political enemies." Abigail immediately defended these appointments as eminently justified, and made without any intention of offense; Mr. Washington had done the same thing at the end of his administration; and, besides, she reminded Mr. Jefferson with delightful frankness, "you will please to recall, Sir, that at the time these appointments were made, there was not any certainty that the presidency would devolve upon you!" It had come very near being Colonel Burr in place of Mr. Jefferson. But Abigail had "never felt any enmity towards you, Sir, for being elected President of the United States," and she could "truly say that at the time of election I considered your pretensions much superior to his who shared an equal vote with you." But since Mr. Jefferson had brought up the subject, Abigail was prepared to "disclose to you what has severed the bonds of former friendship." Mr. Jefferson had remitted the fine of a certain Callender, convicted of libel against Mr. Adams, and this was a public insult to Mr. Adams; and Mr. Jefferson had appointed someone to a judicial post held by John Quincy Adams, and this was a gratuitous manifestation of ill will towards her son which Abigail was much too human to forget. But Mr. Jefferson replied again, defending himself and denying any personal motives in these matters; and so this very honest correspondence, this setting forth of old misunderstandings and griefs, continued for a time, until at the end Abigail wrote that——

"I bear no malice. I cherish no enmity . . . I wish to lead a tranquil and retired life . . . disposed to heal the wounds of contention, to cool the raging fury of party animosity, to soften the rugged spirit of resentment. . . . "

She wished to lead a tranquil and retired life. That was in 1804, and for fourteen years thereafter she was permitted to do so. With her old pet dog Juno at her heels, she went from room to room satisfying her active curiosity concerning all the details of her housekeeping; she made sure that Mr. Adams's tankard of hard cider was ready for him every morning before breakfast; she watched him busying himself in the fields among the hay makers; in her silk gowns covered with lace, she sat impressively at the head of her dinner table dispensing the unfailing corn meal pudding, while the Ex-President bantered his guests with the joviality of mellowing age; she drove about the Massachusetts countryside in a plain carriage and pair, thinking, perhaps, of the days when she had gone to court in a coach, with plumes in her hair. She always received and answered a great many letters.

The years passed. She saw John Quincy return from his ambassadorship to Russia, she saw him appointed Secretary of State, a former Federalist turned Republican, a Montague among the Capulets. But she was not to see him installed as President—thus ironically bearing out the old Republican complaint that John Adams had hoped to establish a dynasty—for on October 28, 1818, she died, of typhoid, in her seventy-fourth year.

Dolly Madison

DOLLY MADISON

1

IN 1768, when Quaker Friend John Payne and his wife, Mary Coles, came trundling back in their coach along the muddy Virginia roads to their home in Hanover County, they brought with them a new baby to show to Mother Amy, the colored nurse. She had been born on May 20, in North Carolina, where her parents were visiting relatives, and christened Dorothea, which immediately became Dolly—or, as they spelled it, Dolley.

She was the first girl in a family of several children, to be followed in time by three other sisters, Lucy, Anna and Mary. A little Quaker girl descended from Scotch and Irish Virginia ancestry—Hanover County on both sides—a little girl with blue eyes twinkling behind long lashes, and the most delicately beautiful pink and white complexion, and a shock of black curls struggling out from under her Quaker bonnet. A gay little Quaker girl, for all her demure behavior; a frivolous little Quaker girl, who hankered

after ribbons, and baubles, and other worldly fripper-
ies; a petted little Quaker girl, who was allowed to
cherish her lovely complexion and preserve it from the
sun under a linen mask worn over her face when she
walked abroad.

The Paynes were well connected, sufficiently prosperous, small planters; the home in Hanover County
was spacious, furnished with brick outbuildings and
"monumental marble mantels," as Dolly remembered
them afterwards. And while the Quaker character
of the house forbade festivity, shunned amusement
and frowned upon the world's vanities, dressing its
inmates in a simplicity of gray—still, there was no
law against abundant good cheer and the broad hospitality of the stately Colony.

Dolly was not taught to dance—she did not dance
at her own Inaugural Ball—she probably did not
take part in the noisy, dusty jollity of county fairs,
where bears were baited, and men and women sat in
grinning contests, and one might view the waxwork
of the Prodigal Son; the candle-lit, brocaded, peri-
wigged gaiety, tremulous with fiddles, of levees, routs
and balls was not permitted her as she grew up; but
all the household mysteries of kitchen and pantry,
of china cupboard, linen closet and wine cellar, of
garden and orchard—these, and perhaps little else
besides, were the very foundation of her education.
Occasionally she may have played Button, Button

with other children, and there must have been dolls, rag dolls, Indian dolls. The rest of the time she sewed, she cooked, she preserved; she knew how to take a mixture of rum, pumpkin beer and brown sugar, dip a hot poker in it, and make flip. She could cipher as well as the next little girl; she spelled no worse than most.

And then in the turbulent revolutionary seventies, when the drums came rolling through Virginia, John Payne—Quaker though he was, and remained—shouldered his musket with the rest and was gone to the war. He came back restless, uneasy, dissatisfied with existence as he saw it in the Dominion. High living, cock fighting, horse racing, rum spilling Virginia was too gay, too dissipated, too flagrantly ungodly for his taste. He longed to find himself in a community more congenial to his sect, in the more austere society of Friends. After a preliminary visit to Philadelphia, he returned to Hanover County to dispose of his property and free his slaves—all but Mother Amy, who would not hear of such an arrangement—and in July, 1783, he settled with his family in the pleasant city of his choice.

2

It was the largest city in the country, with a population of thirty-two thousand, the most fashionable, the most extravagant and the most orderly. A city in which stoops were washed on Wednesdays and Saturdays in all weathers, famous for the excellence of its pavements, the beauty of its brick residences, and the elegance of its citizens—even though there were too many dead cats and dogs in the roadways, a plague of flies in the air, and a multitude of bed-bugs—so it was averred by visiting foreigners—in every corner. A gay city given over to Assemblies, at which ladies over eighteen and gentlemen not under twenty drew their partners by lot and danced passe-pieds and sarabands; a city in which society went to the theatre—in spite of Quaker misgivings —to see *The Prince of Parthia,* and in which ladies read *Peregrine Pickle* and *Roderick Random* while the civic authorities were prohibiting the exhibition of an indecent statue called the Venus de' Medici. A wealthy city, steeped in trade and in the profitable commerce of ships.

And if they took no part in the Assemblies, and abstained from the contaminating influences of the drama, there was no more active and prominent an element of the community to be found in the city's mercantile pursuits than the Quakers—great banking and shipping families, numbered among the most esteemed in Philadelphia's merchant aristocracy, which welcomed John Payne of Virginia and made him one of themselves. John Payne and his whole family, and in particular his daughter Dolly, who brought a loveliness and charm to Evening Meeting which went forth irrepressibly to warm even the most severe of Quaker hearts, just as her black curls were forever escaping from the confinement of her Quaker bonnet.

But in Dolly's mind there were other things in Philadelphia more engrossing than the routine of Meeting, and the decorous diversions to be obtained from country jaunts and simple boating parties. Dolly was fifteen; there was music and tea drinking at Gray's Garden under the trees—and the younger generation of Quakers were beginning to demand toleration for such amusements—and there was Chestnut Street. Chestnut Street where all the fashionable world promenaded in the late afternoon; gentlemen in gold laced cocked hats, and striped stockings and powdered hair; ladies with implanted teeth—Doctor La Mayeur's transplanting process was all the rage—wearing hooped taffetas and flowered brocades, satin petticoats, calash bonnets, and enormous feathered hats. This was Philadelphia, this was life, brilliant and fascinating—the shops, the clothes, the beautiful stuffs, the monumental wigs, the jewels, and all the gaiety and gossip of the town. Under her Quaker gown, Dolly's heart yearned, frankly and without any shame, for these things.

And yet, when they told her to marry John Todd,

she stood up dutifully at "first" and "second Meeting" and proclaimed her willingness to do so. His father was an eminent Quaker school-teacher, he himself was a prominent young lawyer, twenty-seven years old. "I confess I do not admire contention in any form, either political or civil," she once explained. She did not contend against John Todd. It was the first indication, perhaps, of a temperament which she exhibited throughout her life, an ability to accept whatever fate might offer and make the very best of it, always in a complete serenity of spirit.

"There is nothing in this world really worth caring for," she said on another occasion. Nothing mattered enough to make a fuss over it. This attitude may well have been the key to her success.

They were married on January 7, 1790, at the Friends' Meeting House on Pine Street, standing together on the women's side. A very brief, simple ceremony, after which they went quietly to dinner at John Payne's.

3

Three years passed in the placid Todd home on Fourth Street. Dolly's sister Lucy married George Steptoe Washington, the President's nephew, and went to live at Harewood, in Jefferson County, Virginia. John Payne died, after a disastrous business venture which reduced Mrs. Payne to the necessity of taking in boarders. Dolly's first child, John Payne Todd, was born, on February 29, 1792, and the second, William Temple Todd, during the spring of 1793.

And then it was perhaps well that nothing in this world was really worth caring for—for with the summer of 1793 there came the yellow plague, and Dolly was struggling with the children along the crowded road to Gray's Ferry, one of that panic driven throng escaping from the stricken city. John Todd stayed behind, to give his able bodied and courageous help, and before the frosts had purified the air Mr. and Mrs. Todd Senior were dead, and Dolly had lost her husband and her baby. Dolly herself was desperately ill—for she had caught the fever from John when he came staggering out at last to Gray's Ferry —but she recovered to find herself a widow at twenty-five, and executrix of her husband's will in which he had called her "the dear wife of my bosom and first and only woman upon whom my all and only affections were placed."

She came back, in the fall, to her mother's house, the select boarding house as it now was. Philadelphia had become the seat of Government, the town was crowded beyond its capacity with Congressmen and Senators, the inns were inadequate and miserable. Even the famous Indian Queen was only a "pit" which was "Hades, and Tartarus, and Periphlegethon, Cocytus and Styx"—in short, Hell. Mrs. Payne was a gentlewoman, her table was kept in the bountiful Virginia style, her house was probably renowned, if only for the fact of the beautiful Dolly's presence. At all events, the Senator from New York, Colonel Aaron Burr, lodged there. And everywhere, at Oeller's Tavern and at the Coffee House, at the Queen and in the halls of Congress, he told everyone about the pretty widow Todd. He finally told his friend, Congressman Madison of Virginia. The Congressman was very busy; he had good reasons to dislike the fair sex—ever since that unfortunate occasion, ten years before, when he had been jilted by sixteen-year-old Catherine Floyd who sent him back his broken engagement sealed with a lump of dough. But one day he saw the widow Todd driving by; not very long afterwards he was pestering Colonel Burr for an introduction.

"Aaron Burr says that the great little Madison has asked to be brought to me this evening," Dolly wrote to a friend, on a certain day in the spring of 1794, and went to prepare her mulberry satin gown and white scarf in which to receive him.

The great little Madison was forty-three years old; a man who had served with distinction in the Continental Congress, the Virginia Legislature and the Constitutional Convention, who had helped produce the *Federalist* and was spoken of as the Father of the Constitution, and who was now a member of the House of Representatives, thanks to Mr. Patrick Henry who had kept him out of the Senate. A dapper, timid, studious little light haired man in black clothes, who could be quite entertaining when you got him off by himself. Not at all the sort of person who should have attracted Dolly Todd, or, for that matter, have been attracted to her. But timid and little as he was, she saw that he was indeed great, and she liked him. It was not long before their engagement was rumored all over Philadelphia. Jim Madison and the widow Todd. Mrs. Washington sent for her kinswoman by marriage and catechised her on the subject. Was it true that she was going to marry Mr. Madison, because if so the President and Mrs. Washington most heartily approved—a point which may or may not have been keeping Dolly awake nights. But Dolly was not sure. In August she wrote to her lawyer, Mr. William Wilkins, and asked him what he thought. And Mr. Wilkins replied that—

"Mr. M—n is a man whom I admire. I know his attachment to you and did not therefore content myself with taking his character from the breath of popular applause—but consulted those who knew him intimately in private life. His private character therefore I have every reason to believe is good and amiable. He unites to the great talents which have secured his public approbation those engaging qualities that contribute so highly to domestic felicity. . . . You have my fullest and freest approbation of the step you are about to take. . . ."

And so they were married, on September 15, 1794, at Harewood, her sister's residence. A very fine wedding, with dancing and feasting this time, during which the bridesmaids cut up Mr. Madison's ruffles of Mechlin lace as keepsakes.

John Todd had not been dead a year. . . .

4

They drove in their coach to Montpellier, the Madison home in Orange County, Virginia, to see father and mother Madison, and then they were back in Philadelphia, on Spruce Street, for the session of Congress.

And now there was a new Philadelphia for Quaker Dolly, the Philadelphia that she had always longed for. The fashionable promenade on Chestnut Street —or rather on the north side of Market now, between Third and Fifth—was hers on which to display the feathered finery which even a Quaker lady might indulge in when she was the wife of the great little Madison. In her house she had furniture of maple, no doubt, and chairs with horsehair seats, English carpets, and a profusion of silver on the sideboards.

She breakfasted elegantly at nine of the morning,
on ham, salt fish, bread and butter, and tea. For
dinner in the afternoon she served soup and several
kinds of meat, cabbage in thin slices, pastries and
puddings, and the best claret and madeira. In the
early evening people came to supper and ate oysters,
while she filled the teacups over and over again, until
the guests signified their refusal by turning them up-
side down in the accepted manner.

The town had never been more gay—crowded with
carriages, resonant with the gossip of routs and balls,
stately with dinners at which were gathered all the
official aristocracy of the land—a continually chang-
ing pageant of foreign guests and Ministers, a brilliant scene, graced, moreover, by the presence of
many of the emigrated nobility of France. In her
new rôle, as Mrs. Madison of Montpellier, Dolly
plunged into these festivities with all the stored-up
zest of her restrained girlhood. For three years she
brought a fresh, bright personality to enliven Lady
Washington's somewhat stuffy levees in the old brick
house on Market Street; with her dear friend Sally
McKean—the beautiful, vivacious Sally, daughter
of Chief Justice McKean, who was to become the
bride of the Spanish Minister, Don Carlos, Marquis
de Yrujo—she watched Mr. Washington driving by
in his scarlet paneled coach with the white horses;
she attended the Assemblies at Oeller's Tavern, in the

big room decorated with French republican wall paper, and looked on while the ladies called the dances in turn and the Managers saw to it that no gentleman presented himself in "boots, colored stockings or undress;" for three years—while the more sober minded of her sect smiled tolerantly at their daughter's unorthodoxies—she made friends in all camps for Jim Madison.

And Jim Madison did not care for it; all these routs and levees, all this pother of gossip and flirtation, all this commotion of dinners and balls; and he would have resigned his seat, and retired to his beloved Montpellier, to his solitude and his books. But they would not, they could not, let him go. Little Madison was too great a man in the councils of the Republic.

"Present me respectfully to Mrs. Madison," Mr. Jefferson wrote, "and pray her to keep you where you are, for her own satisfaction and for the public good."

And for the public good, no doubt, but certainly for her own satisfaction, she did so—until a new administration in 1797, with Federalist Mr. Adams in the President's chair, sent them home for four years, to Montpellier at last. Except for a passing visit or two—a sojourn under the great Doctor Physick's care, caused by an injury to her knee, and a journey to New York many years later—Dolly's Philadelphia days were done.

5

And on the morning of March 4, 1801, crowds stood in front of Conrad's boarding house, in Washington City, to catch a glimpse of Mr. Jefferson. Mr. Adams had gone rattling out of town the night before in his coach; the Federalists were defeated; in a few moments, the Mammoth of Democracy was to take his place as President of the United States—the first to be inaugurated in the Federal City.

Conrad's—built originally as a residence by Mr. Thomas Law, and placed by him as a boarding house at the disposal of members of Congress assembled in that unfinished city, that village in a dusty wilderness, in which there was nothing to be seen "save brick kilns and laborers' huts"—stood on the south side of Capitol Hill.

"It was on top of the hill, the precipitous sides of which were covered with grass, shrubs and trees in their wild uncultivated state. Between the foot of the hill and the broad Potomac extended a wide plain, through which the Tiber wound its way. The romantic beauty of this little stream was not then deformed by wharves or other works of art. Its banks were shaded with tall and umbrageous forest trees of every variety, among which the superb tulip poplar rose conspicuous; the magnolia, the azalia, the hawthorn, the wild rose and many other indigenous shrubs grew beneath their shade, while violets, anemonies and a thousand other sweet wood flowers found shelter among their roots. . . . The wild grape vine climbing from tree to tree hung in unpruned luxuriance among the branches of the trees and formed a fragrant and verdant canopy over the greensward, impervious to the noonday sun."

Aside from that, Washington was not a pretty place, or an agreeable place, nor yet a healthy one, with its malarial marshes. Nothing was ready; long, cheerless, empty vistas stretched between public edifices scattered about at inconvenient distances; the city's squares, according to Tom Moore, were still morasses, its only obelisks the trees in its encircling forests; the President's House, situated on barren ground separated from the Capitol by impassable swamps, was incomplete, and surrounded by piles of rubbish; Mrs. Adams had only recently been using its audience chamber as a drying room for laundry. But the place had become the seat of Government; the House of Representatives must convene there, the Senate, the diplomatic corps with many groans —General Turreau from France, who wore diamonds and beat his wife; the Marquis de Yrujo from Spain, who surpassed them all in the matter of gorgeous apparel; Mr. Anthony Merry from England, and his tall, mannish lady, whom Mr. Jefferson called a virago, possibly because she thought him a boor—and the members of the Cabinet must live there.

And so, as soon as the death of his father made it

possible, Secretary of State Madison—they had dragged him away from Montpellier again—and his wife came to reside in Washington, in Mr. Voss's house on F Street. And because Mr. Jefferson was fond of them both, and because he was a widower whose married daughters, Martha Randolph and Polly Eppes, were away in Virginia most of the time and the President's House consequently without a lady to do its honors, Mrs. Secretary of State Madison found herself presiding at the head of the Executive board, receiving all officialdom in the parlors of the Great House—such of them as were habitable —and supervising the republican amenities of that socially somewhat abrupt administration.

For while politically the new President was engrossed in the task of putting the ship of state on her "republican tack," it became immediately evident, also, that the social formalities of the previous régime were to be abandoned for a more democratic simplicity of deportment, a less meticulous observance of former rigidities of etiquette as practised by the Federalist Presidents. In fact, they were not to be observed at all. In spite of the ladies of Washington, who attempted to force their continuance by appearing uninvited at the Great House on the customary day, Mr. Jefferson promptly abolished the weekly levees of the "court," and, in the same breath, did away with precedence. A perfect equality, he pro-

claimed, was to exist between the guests at all public
and private dinners, and " . . . to give force to the
principle of equality or pele mele"—a principle
highly distasteful to Mrs. Minister Merry, for instance, who resented the spectacle of Mrs. Madison
being taken into dinner by the President, while
she herself was left to crowd her way through
the door as best she might on the arm of her own
husband—"and to prevent the growth of precedence
out of courtesy, the members of the Executive at their
own houses will adhere to the ancient usage of their
ancestors—gentlemen *en masse* giving place to the
ladies *en masse.*"   It was to be noted, however, in
the midst of all this *pele mele en masse* republican
simplicity, that "the President and his family take
precedence everywhere, in public or private."

Mrs. Merry and her humorless husband—and the
Marquis de Yrujo, for political reasons of his own—
were not inclined to accept this Jeffersonian hurly
burly without protest, and for some time the Washington teacups were agitated by the most violent
of diplomatic tempests, which ran its course in a perfect gale of hearty American laughter. But Mr. Jefferson was not moved; either by Mrs. Merry whom
he detested; or by Dolly Madison who strove to miti-
gate the more ungraceful aspects of the new era.
Mr. Jefferson remained incorrigible.   He persisted
in appearing publicly in thick, hairy waistcoats and

insecure woollen stockings; he would give audiences
to foreign Ministers in dilapidated slippers, and scabrous red undervests and green velveteen breeches;
he lounged, he shambled, he spread his ungainly, loose
jointed limbs upon the adjacent furniture; to many,
he presented a picture of unnecessarily plebeian clum-
siness, utterly without dignity and presence.

But he gave excellent dinners, no matter how one
went in to them. There were eleven servants at the
"Palace"—as the Federalists dubbed it—a French
cook and a French steward. There was company,
usually a dozen, every day, and they sat at table from
four o'clock in the afternoon until well on in the evening, enjoying a very considerable *pele mele* of refreshments.

"Dined at the President's," Senator Mitchill records. "Rice soup, round of beef, turkey, mutton,
ham, loin of veal, cutlets of mutton or veal, fried
eggs, fried beef"—and a curious dish which stumped
the Senator—" a pie called macaroni, which appeared
to be a rich crust filled with the strillions of onions, or
shallots, which I took it to be, tasted very strong and
not very agreeable. . . . Ice cream, very good, crust
wholly dried, crumbled into thin flakes; a dish somewhat like a pudding—inside white as milk or curd,
very porous and light, covered with cream sauce—
very fine. Many other jimcracks, a great variety of
fruit, plenty of wines and good."

There was no precedence at the President's table, but the wines were always plentiful and excellent. And if Mr. Jefferson had occasion to disagree publicly with the Marquis de Yrujo on sundry questions of international policy, in the matter of vintages they were, apparently, in perfect accord.

"Dear Sir," Mr. Jefferson once wrote to the Collector of the Port at Philadelphia, "Mons. d'Yrujo, the Spanish Minister here, has been so kind as to spare me two hundred bottles of champagne, part of a larger parcel imported for his own use, and consequently privileged from duty; but it would be improper for me to take the benefit of that. I must therefore ask the favor of you to take the proper measures for paying the duty; for which purpose I enclose you a bank check for twenty-two and a half dollars, the amount of it. If it could be done without mentioning my name, it would avoid ill intended observations."

A conclusion perhaps characteristic of that most prudent of Presidents.

6

For eight years, "Queen Dolly," as they called her, ruled over the social destinies of the Executive Mansion, in spite of the demands upon her strength and the humidity of the malarial marshes which crippled her with inflammatory rheumatism from which she suffered all the rest of her life.

In the summers there were frequent visits to Monticello—and a special chamber set aside for them there, known as the Madison room—and there was Montpellier, and an endless stream of guests, fifteen and twenty at a time, rolling up uninvited and unexpected, and always welcome in the good Virginia fashion. In the winters there were gaieties and functions; Dolly's sister Anna came to live with them, and married Mr. Richard Cutts; the President's daughters were there occasionally, Dolly's great friend Martha, and the beautiful Polly whom she admired so much; there were gowns and wigs—monumental, pyramidical, five dollar wigs—to be procured at Philadelphia; there were horse races and games of brag and loo, although Dolly finally renounced gambling at cards; there was a brilliant, cosmopolitan society for all the crude simplicity of its surroundings; there were receptions and balls, attended by the beautiful young ladies of Georgetown, at which "one danced and sang sentimental songs;" and there were scandals.

"I am half tempted," Mrs. Samuel Harrison Smith wrote to her sister in 1804, "to enter into details of our city affairs and personages, but really I shall have to be so scandalous that I am afraid of amusing you at such a risk." What a pity! However, concerning a certain well known lady she thought it no harm to speak the truth.

"She has made a great noise here and mobs of boys
have crowded round her splendid equipage to see
what I hope will not often be seen in this country, an
almost naked woman. An elegant and select party
was given to her by Mrs. Robt. Smith; her appearance was such that it threw all the company into confusion, and no one dared to look at her but by stealth;
the window shutters being left open, a crowd assembled round the windows to get a look at this beautiful
little creature. . . . Her dress was the thinnest sar-
cenet and white crepe without the least stiffening in
it . . . there was scarcely any waist to it and no
sleeves; her back, her bosom, part of her waist, and
her arms were uncovered, and the rest of her form
visible. She was engaged the next evening at Madm.
P's; Mrs. R. Smith and several other ladies sent her
word, if she wished to meet them there she must promise to have more clothes on."

Dolly was in the midst of it all; she had "good humor and sprightliness, united to the most affable and
agreeable manners"; she had tact and charity, and
endless common sense; she was frank, and hearty,
and simple, and always accessible. People liked her,
she was good fun; she attracted to her the men of all
political faiths, and made them her friends—and
Madison's, as she called him—in her home there were
no parties, no factions, there was simply a brilliant
gathering of notable personages, and Queen Dolly.
She was not brilliant herself, not intellectually re-

markable, not a wit. Her letters are almost entirely
concerned with an infinity of unimportant little matters; she had nothing noteworthy to say about the
great events and issues of her time. Hamilton was
killed and she talked about glassware; Burr was captured and "we are quiet and have but few parties."
It was one of her "sources of happiness never to desire a knowledge of other people's business." She
was not interested in their business, only in their personality.

It was, in part, a deliberate attitude. In 1804
already, she was "learning to hold my tongue well;"
in 1805, while she was "extremely anxious to hear
what is going forward in the Cabinet," still she was
"not much of a politician," and she believed that her
husband would not desire his wife "to be the active
partisan that our neighbor, Mrs. L., is; nor will there
be the slightest danger, while she is conscious of her
want of talents, and the diffidence in expressing
those opinions always imperfectly understood by her
sex."

It was, to a certain extent, deliberate, but much of
it was the result, one suspects, of temperament. Dolly
took life as she found it; her husband was in Mr.
Jefferson's party, and she was intensely Republican
—if he had been a Federalist she would have been
just as intensely Federalist. She had no consuming
convictions of that sort; great events were simply

accidents which caused a change of domicile, a shifting of faces at her dinner table; she had no fundamental interest in politics, except as they influenced the career of her Madison.   Those were matters for the men to rant over—for herself, she was content to discharge her social duties, to make his home the shrine of contemporary society, to be a great lady. In these respects, she had, perhaps, no equal in her day.   She was, of course, a tremendous, an incalculable help to him, as Secretary and as President—and she had a tremendously good time doing it.

Although, from a domestic standpoint, it was not an easy task.   Servants were most unsatisfactory; in Mrs. Smith's home, for instance, there was an old woman in the kitchen, a drudge who could not cook, there was a "miserable, idle, dirty girl" as a waiter, there was Milly, the "standbye," who cleaned the house, made the beds, ironed and clear starched, and there was "a fine little girl of five years old bound to me by Doctor Willis," who played with the baby. Mrs. Smith spent two or three hours in the kitchen every day, and prepared and even dished up every dinner eaten by the family.   All the mornings and evenings she sewed, but the interruptions—and they were probably more frequent at Dolly's—from company and family calls were so numerous that her work was always behind hand.

"It is," she complained, "so entirely the custom to visit of a morning here, that if we keep up any intercourse with society our mornings are most of them sacrificed. Of an evening some one or more of the gentlemen of Congress are always here. . . . An unprofitable way of life, but there is no alternative in this place between gay company and parties, and perfect solitude."

There was never any question of solitude at Dolly's and while she probably did not cook them herself, she gave bountiful afternoon dinners which Mrs. Merry thought were more like harvest home suppers. They were usually "bouilli," with spices and herbs in the dish and a rich gravy; there was cabbage, "much boiled, then cut in long strings and somewhat mashed;" there was a large ham, and other meats, a good dessert with "two dishes which appeared like apple pie in the form of the half of a musk-melon, the flat side down, top creased deep, and the color a dark brown;" and there were Madison's excellent port and madeira. . . .

7

And then, in March, 1809, Mr. Jefferson retired, smiling, to Monticello, Mr. Madison inevitably became President, and Dolly moved into that Great House of which she had already been mistress so long. And if the barbers of Washington bemoaned the elevation to the presidency of "this little Jim Madison with a queue no bigger than a pipe stem," the inaugural ceremonies were none the less brilliant and impressive. There were processions, and troops, and salutes; there was a great reception at Mrs. Madison's, who, in a beautiful bonnet of purple velvet and white satin with plumes, was "all dignity, grace and affability;" and there was a grand ball at Long's Hotel, concerning which Mr. John Quincy Adams was of the opinion that "the crowd was excessive, the heat oppressive, and the entertainment bad." But the other three hundred and ninety-nine persons who were present thought it most respectable and elegant; and as for Her Majesty—

"She looked a Queen. She had on a pale, buff colored velvet made plain, with a very long train but not the least trimming—a beautiful pearl necklace, earrings and bracelet—her head-dress was a turban of the same colored velvet and white satin—from Paris, with two superb plumes of the bird of paradise feathers." Quaker Dolly! "It would be absolutely impossible for anyone to behave with more perfect propriety than she did. Unassuming dignity, sweetness, grace . . . such manners would disarm envy itself and conciliate even enemies."

There followed years of stately gaiety, a restoration of graceful pomps at the President's House—the "Castle," as that era knew it—a pageantry of four horse chariots and gilded ambassadorial coaches, a perpetual round of re-established levees and "drawing rooms." The House was still unfinished, poorly furnished in spite of belated Congressional expenditures, but there were mirrors, and in Dolly's parlor upholsteries of yellow satin, and festoons of valanced damask, and highbacked chairs and sophas. Mr. Gallatin came there, and Mr. James Monroe, George Clinton, Calhoun, John Randolph, Henry Clay, John Marshall, and their ladies; Dolly and her famous sisters, Anna Cutts and Lucy Washington, were to be seen everywhere together; Mrs. John P. Van Ness gave parties. Washington was coming into its own, blessed with "more attractions than any other place in America."

"There are here," Mrs. Smith found, "peculiar facilities for forming acquaintances. . . . The House of Representatives is the lounging place of both sexes where acquaintance is as easily made as at public amusements. And the drawing room— that centre of attractions—affords opportunity of seeing all those whom fashion, fame, beauty, wealth or talents have rendered celebrated. . . . The debates in Congress have this winter been very attractive to the ladies." As for the Supreme Court, "a place in which I think women have no business, the effect of female admiration and attention has been very obvious, but it is a doubt to me whether it has been beneficial. . . . A member told me he doubted not there had been much more speaking on this account, and another gentleman told me that one day Mr. Pinckney had finished his argument and was just about seating himself, when Mrs. Madison and a train of ladies entered—he recommenced, went over the same ground, using fewer arguments, but scattering more flowers. . . . " In fact, "the women here are taking a station in society which is not known elsewhere. On every public occasion . . . in the court, in the representative hall, as well as the drawing room, they are treated with marked distinction."

In other respects, Mrs. Smith thought—

"the manners here different from those in other places. At the drawing room, at our parties, few ladies ever sit. Our rooms are always so crowded, that few more could find a place in the rooms; the consequence is the ladies and gentlemen stand and walk about the rooms, in mingled groups, which certainly produces more ease, freedom and equality. . . . "

There, perhaps, was the keynote of the administration—more ease, freedom and equality, adorned with a very considerable elegance. The President was "a little man with powdered hair, having an abstracted air and a pale countenance, with but little flow of courtesy;" he labored incessantly, his face was "pallid and hard," and although he appeared daily in society, he only relaxed "towards the end of a protracted dinner with confidential friends," when he became "anecdotal, facetious, a little broad occasionally in his discourse, after the manner of the old school."

"Jemmy Madison," so Mr. Washington Irving sized him up. "Ah, poor Jemmy! He is but a withered little apple-John!"

But Dolly was "a fine, portly, buxom dame, who has a smile and a pleasant word for everybody," and her sisters were "like the two Merry Wives of Windsor." She was in her forties now, but young looking, and in the best of spirits; in spite of Friend Rebekah Hubbs, whose "soul's desire for thee is that thou may more and more come out of all that cumbers the earth" and "put away from thee all the fading pleasures of this world," Dolly painted and powdered a little—although the question was hotly argued among contemporaries—she took snuff constantly, from lava and platina boxes, and used large bandanna handkerchiefs.

"This is for rough work," she is once supposed to have explained to Mr. Clay, whereas her little lace handkerchief was merely her "polisher."

She towered above the crowded levees in her rose colored satin robes trimmed with ermine, and her ostrich feathered turbans, and her amethyst ear drops; her honest laughter was always ringing out; perhaps not always so sure of herself, she contrived painstakingly to put everyone at his ease, even the

young gentleman who in his excitement at meeting
her tried to cram a teacup into his pocket—a lady
who always appeared in her parlor with a book in
her hand; not that she ever had leisure to read, but—

". . . in order to have something not ungraceful
to say, and if need be to supply a word of talk."

A cheerful, sweet tempered, gracious, jolly lady;
a charitable lady, who found time to cut out hundreds
of garments for the City Orphan Asylum; a wise,
clever lady in her own appointed ways, who invited
Mrs. Gallatin to represent her at drawing rooms
after the President had quarrelled with Mr. Gallatin,
and who had Mrs. William Seaton to dinner when
her husband became editor of the important *National
Intelligencer,* and who did many little kindnesses
to many people—so that finally Madison was allowed
to have a second term.

8

And in the meantime, there was war. "The world"
—Dolly was moved to so deep a thought—"the world
seems to be running mad, what with one thing and
another." An embargo to begin with, in April, 1812,
which kept ships idle in the ports with protecting
tar barrels at their mastheads—Madison's Night-
caps; and, in June, a war with England, an unpopular war throughout the eastern and middle states—
Madison's War. The "Immortal Twelfth" Con-

gress, filled with young Republican "war hawks" and speakered by Henry Clay, adjourned; in all the toasts at Federalist gatherings Mr. Jefferson was Jeroboam who made Israel to walk in sin, and the President was Nadab, the son of Jeroboam, who walked in his father's way; at Washington—after Bladensburg—a well known Federalist lady drove up to Mrs. Madison's door, arose in her carriage, and, loosening her long and celebrated hair, prayed that an opportunity might be vouchsafed her to sacrifice it as a halter for Mr. Madison.

But still he was re-elected, thanks primarily, perhaps, to Dolly who never lost her head, as a more imaginative person might well have done, "what with one thing and another." In spite of the fiasco of Mr. John Henry's supposedly portentous New England secession letters, which the fascinating Count Edouard de Crillon—who owned vast estates at St. Martial, in Lebeur, near the Spanish border, and who had temporarily incurred the displeasure of Napoleon—had persuaded Secretary of State Monroe to purchase for fifty thousand dollars. And in spite of the Government's, to say nothing of society's, mortifying discovery—after his departure from these shores with official despatches for the American Minister at Paris, and some part, at least, of the gullible John Henry's thousands—that the fascinating de Crillon was not at all a Count, nor did he possess any vast estates at St. Martial, in Lebeur, near the Spanish border, nor yet had he incurred the displeasure of Napoleon, except in so far as he might have fallen short in his capacity as a police spy of the Emperor's.

And the war was not going badly, in spite of Hull at Detroit. For a while, indeed, the country was ringing with victories, splendid victories on the sea. In seven months, the Americans had taken five hundred English merchantmen and three frigates; the "gridiron flag" was doing well. The English papers said so and tried peevishly to explain it. There were bonfires, and a constant tolling of bells, and naval balls—such as the one at Tomlinson's Hotel, at Washington, in celebration of the capture of the *Alert* and the *Guerriere;* in the midst of which Lieutenant Hamilton came stamping into the room, bringing with him the flag of the newly taken *Macedonian* to place at Dolly's feet, with a flourish of trumpets, and a great huzzaing and many "tigers." So the much disputed, and frequently denied, story goes; and it must have been so, for there was a lady present who wrote afterwards that in her opinion Mrs. Madison did not use rouge, since "I am well assured I saw her color come and go at the Naval Ball when the *Macedonian's* flag was presented to her by young Hamilton."

9

And then on Tuesday, August 23, 1814, Mrs. Secretary of the Navy Jones found it necessary to write to Dolly that—

"in the present state of alarm and bustle of preparation for the worst that may happen, I imagine it will be more convenient to dispense with the enjoyment of your hospitality today, and therefore pray you to admit this as an excuse for Mr. Jones, Lucy and myself . . . Lucy and I are packing with the possibility of having to leave."

It was to have been a big dinner for all the Cabinet —a dinner which subsequent legend has placed on the following day, with the viands all on the table and the wine ready in the coolers—but the British fleet was in the Chesapeake, British troops were marching through the woods to Washington, and the Cabinet officers were with the President at General Winder's camp, taking such haphazard measures for the capital's defence as occurred to their improvident minds. As the famous John Gilpin parody recounts—

"Monroe was there, and Armstrong bold,
  No bolder man mote be,
  And Rush, the Attorney Gen-e-ral,
  All on their horses three."

But the British kept right on marching, by the Bladensburg road which no one had thought to obstruct, and instead of dining at Dolly's the Cabinet went streaming across country to Bladensburg with the army, "a motley throng," according to Mr. McMaster, "made up of militia, regulars, volunteers, sailors, generals, secretaries and the President." And on Wednesday, August 24, there was a battle. An unfortunate battle in which the base British fired rockets at the astonished militia, so that they departed in some confusion to their homes, along with the rest of the soldiery—all but the sailors, who conducted themselves with a tenacity as glorious as it was hopeless. As for the secretaries and the President—poor Mr. Madison was no sailor; he had spent his time writing pencil notes to Dolly, and half way through the engagement he came to the conclusion that it would "now be proper for us to retire in the rear, leaving the military movements to military men." He had not, however, foreseen the direction which these movements were so soon to take. It was, in short, a disgraceful afternoon, but as Mrs. Smith explained it later—

"We are naturally a brave people, and it was not so much fear as prudence which caused our retreat. Too late they discovered the dispreparation of our troops." They had certainly not expected to have rockets fired at them.

And at Washington that afternoon there was tumult and clamor in the streets. Dolly scanned the horizon with a spyglass and saw nothing to encourage her—only groups of soldiers hurrying in every direction except to Bladensburg. There was a dust of departing family coaches. In the dining room at the Castle, Paul Jennings had laid the table for Dolly's dinner—a fact no doubt responsible for the legend of the Cabinet function—but she was not to partake of it, and it remained for Admiral Cockburn to find when he entered the city, just as she had "precipitally" left it. Because at three o'clock a messenger came galloping up and she must fly. For the second time in American history, the British were coming! They sent the plate and such movables as could be taken away in a wagon; at Dolly's suggestion, "French" John Siousa and Magrau, the gardener, broke the frame containing Gilbert Stuart's portrait of Mr. Washington, and gave the picture to some gentlemen for safe keeping; Dolly herself passed through the dining room, crammed some things into her reticule, and was then driven to Georgetown in her carriage, with Mr. Carroll and Sukey, her maid; or, according to the ballad—

> "Sister Cutts, and Cutts, and I,
> And Cutts's children three
> Will fill the coach—and you must ride
> On horseback after we!"

The Castle was abandoned; to be raided, first, by
American stragglers—Mrs. Smith is authority for the
statement—who drank up two thousand dollars'
worth of wines in the cellar; and then to be burned
by the British, who "conflagrated" it after marching
fifty sailors and marines silently through the avenue,

"each carrying a long pole to which was fixed a ball
about the circumference of a large plate—when arrived at the building each man was stationed at a
window with his pole and machine of wild fire against
it; at the word of command, at the same instant the
windows were broken and this wild fire thrown in, so
that an instantaneous conflagration took place, and
the whole building was wrapt in flames and smoke."

Mrs. Smith's report of Mrs. Thornton's description
of the episode differs somewhat from the customary
account of ransacked rooms and furniture piled high
to be fired with a picturesque coal brought from a
neighboring tavern. The British burned several
other public buildings, a newspaper office, and some
private houses from which they had been sniped at,
otherwise all the officers and men "were perfectly
polite to the citizens," and Admiral Cockburn "bade
them complain of any soldier that committed the least
disorder." On the other hand—

"Oh, my sister, how gloomy is the scene. I do
not suppose Government will ever return to Wash-

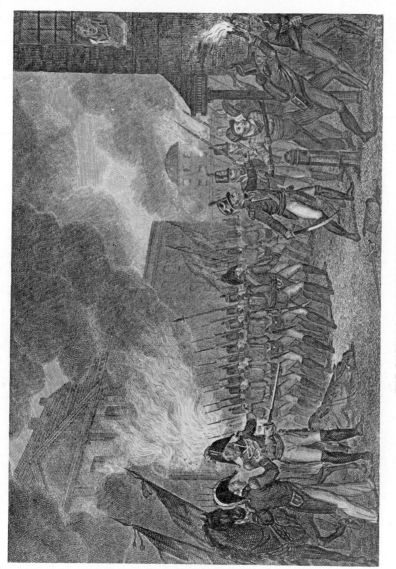

THE BURNING OF WASHINGTON IN 1814

ington. All those whose property was invested in that place will be reduced to poverty!"

But Government did return to Washington, and in a very few days. For there was a terrible hurricane, and the British retired; and after various vicissitudes and discomforts, and a hasty flying from pillar to post—during the course of which Dolly was driven out of one house by an angry matron who screamed at her to come down and go out, because "your husband has got mine out fighting, and damn you, you shan't stay in my house!"—the President, and the Cabinet, and Dolly all found themselves once more in the Federal City. And so—

"Now long live Madison, the brave,
And Armstrong, long live he;
And Rush, and Cutts, Monroe and Jones,
And Dolly, long live she!"

10

The Castle was "conflagrated," only its blackened walls remaining, and after a temporary sojourn at the home of her sister, Mrs. Cutts, Dolly established herself in the Tayloe mansion; the famous brick "Octagon" with the pillared portico adorned with traceries, in the chambers of which—while the Cabinet passed through the circular vestibule and up the white winding stairs to the round boudoir above—

the pomps and amenities of days before the war were soon again in full observance.

For on February 4, 1815, there was news in the streets of victory at New Orleans, and the name of a President-to-be on every tongue; on February 13, an express rider came foaming into town from the North, with tidings of the sloop of war *Favorite* at New York, and an envoy come home bearing articles of peace; and on the next day, in the midst of jubilating bells and guns, Mr. Carroll arrived in person, and there was Peace.

"Peace and Plenty! Peace, Commerce and Prosperity!"

Mr. Gallatin and Mr. Adams, Mr. Clay, Mr. Bayard and Mr. Russell, had made a treaty; to be sure, it carried with it no increase of territory, it said nothing about impressment, it did not refer to the rights of neutrals on the sea—these burning questions which had brought on the war—but there were to be commissions to arbitrate future disputes, and there was Peace, a hundred years and more of Peace, could they but have realized it. The whole town went to Mrs. Madison's; someone was ringing a dinner bell; someone else thought to tell the domestics. "Peace! Peace!" Down in the servants' hall there was wine, and Paul Jennings played the President's March on the violin, and "French" John Siousa got very drunk.

It was a gay winter, that "Peace Winter" of 1815;

one brilliant gathering after another spread its tur-
baned and gold laced splendors across the presidential drawing rooms at the Octagon, and, later, in the
mansion on Pennsylvania Avenue where Mrs. Madison sat "with Mrs. Monroe, Mrs. Decatur and a dozen
other ladies in a formidable row;" the last years of
Madison's presidency came and went, with Dolly
queening it as perhaps never before; and then it was
March, 1817, and Mr. Monroe was to have his turn,
and the play was done.

"You are," Supreme Court Justice Johnson wrote
to Dolly, "about to enter upon the enjoyment of the
most enviable state which can fall to the lot of man-
kind—to carry with you to your retirement the bless-
ings of all who ever knew you. Think not, Madam,
that I address to you the language of flattery. . . .
And be assured that all who have ever enjoyed the
honor of your acquaintance will long remember that
polite condescension which never failed to encourage
the diffident, that suavity of manner which tempted
the morose or thoughtful to be cheerful, or that benevolence of aspect which suffered no one to turn from
you without an emotion of gratitude. . . . "

11

And now there was nothing but Montpellier, and
the calm, monotonous beauty of the Blue Ridge.
Madison was sixty-six, his mother—wonderful Nellie
Madison, alert and occupied, with her knitting and her

ancient books—was eighty-five, Dolly was only forty-nine. After the Castle and the Octagon, after the dazzling pageant of sixteen magnificent Washington seasons, after the music, and the laughter, and the companionable hubbub of crowded drawing rooms, there was a quiet, slightly dilapidated, colonaded mansion against a background of unchanging trees, there were some rooms "furnished with French carpets, large windows, a good many paintings, and some statuary—altogether without any fashionable or very elegant equipment, yet in a gentlemanlike style of rural prosperity;" there was a path lined with box, and a garden.

There—with the exception of one brief visit to Washington—Dolly was to spend the next twenty years, quite cheerfully and serenely, with "all the elegance and polish of fashion, the unadulterated simplicity, freshness, warmth and friendliness of her native character and native state." She was still "one of the happiest of human beings," she seemed to have "no place about her which could afford a lodgement for care or trouble;" she looked young and felt so, and received "a succession of visitors, among whom . . . a great many foreigners"—sometimes as many as "ninety persons to dine with us at one table fixed on the lawn," at a banquet which was "profuse and handsome, and the company very orderly." Twenty years; ministering to Mother Madison until her death,

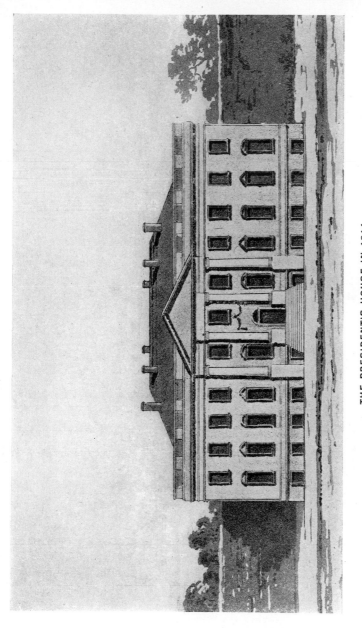

THE PRESIDENT'S HOUSE IN 1814

From an engraving published in 1814 by G. and S. Robinson

in 1829; reading to Madison when his eyes began to
fail, and asking that novels less melodramatic than
those of Mr. Cooper be sent to her; enduring the
pains of rheumatism and the tribulation of her own
weakening eyesight; listening—after the first welcome days of rest, perhaps a little wistfully but never
impatiently—to the echoes that came drifting to
her from the world which she had loved so well.

And then the accumulating years brought separation and sorrow; the dear friend at Monticello passed
away in 1826, Mr. Monroe died in 1831, Dolly's sister, Anna Cutts, in 1832, and at last, in 1836, Madison himself. Dolly was very sick afterwards; however, a visit to the White Sulphur, in 1837, did her
good; they sent her niece, Anna Payne, to her to keep
her company; and she found something to occupy her
in the editing and publishing of her husband's Reports of the Constitutional Congress. But she was
sixty-nine now—for Dolly, nothing remained, surely,
but the lonely contemplation of fading scenes. . . .

12

Not at all. Back there in the world people were
still attending receptions, carriages were still rolling
by to drawing rooms, there were still music, and
laughter, and the same companionable hubbub to be
heard. Dolly went back. In 1837, with her niece,

to the old Cutts house on "President's Square," in friendly, welcoming Washington.

It was a new Washington in many ways, new Brussels carpets and chandeliers, green blinds and red and white curtains at every window, new manners, new names, new faces. But all this new Washington, and all that was left of the old, seemed ennobled and more stately for her coming, and turned to her with respectful affection. The "venerable Mrs. Madison"—for they always supposed her to be older than she was, forgetting how much younger than her husband she had been; Mrs. Madison, in her old fashioned gowns and turbans; in her favorite black velvet with the leg of mutton sleeves, and the open bosom filled with white tulle rising to a ruff about her face, a bright Roman shawl around her shoulders; Mrs. Madison, "the Dowager," whom all the town visited on state occasions, who went everywhere and saw everything—she was aboard the *Princeton* when the disastrous explosion took place—who held her court as graciously and sweetly as ever in other days; a cherished old lady who was still "eminently beautiful, with a complexion as fresh and fair, and a skin as smooth, as that of an English girl."

"A young lady of fourscore years and upwards," Mr. Philip Hone was exaggerating a little, "goes to parties and receives company like the queen of this new world."

Although it was not always so easy now to maintain the old standards of Virginia hospitality, the old abundant table. Congress had paid for Mr. Madison's Reports, but Montpellier itself had to be sold, finally, for there was always John Payne Todd, the scapegrace son, with his debts, and his scrapes, and his heartrending neglect of his mother—he who was himself so negligible. But Washington did not neglect her; they sent her baskets of fruit and provisions, little gifts which she might accept as tokens of the deeply rooted esteem in which she was held. And Congress did not forget her, but placed in trust for her the sum expended for the purchase of Mr. Madison's letters, and gave her the franking privilege, and a seat on the floor of the House during her lifetime. For she was more than the venerable Mrs. Madison—she was a national treasure, a precious relic of the past, a very great lady to whom little children were brought.

And then, in 1849, President Polk, recording in his diary the incidents of his last levee at the White House, wrote that—

"All the parlours, including the East Room, were lighted up. The Marine Band of Musicians occupied the outer hall. Many hundreds of persons, ladies and gentlemen, attended. It was what would be called in the society of Washington a very fashionable levee. Foreign Ministers, their families and suites; Judges, members of both Houses of Congress, and many citizens and strangers were of the company present. I stood and shook hands with them for near three hours. Towards the close of the evening I passed through the crowded rooms with the venerable Mrs. Madison on my arm."

A very fashionable levee, all the parlors lighted up, a brilliant company, crowded rooms, and Mrs. Madison passing towards the close of the evening. All the things that she had loved, that she had done so much to grace; music, laughter and a companionable hubbub; those reconstructed chambers of the Castle, a President of the United States at her side; a splendid fitness to the scene such as seldom glorifies human events. Mrs. Madison passing—did they, perhaps, suspect it, as they bowed her out with tender courtesy —for the last time.

It was February 7; Dolly was at the close of her eightieth year, she was in white satin, with the inevitable turban—and on July 12 she died.

Elizabeth Monroe and Louisa Adams

ELIZABETH MONROE AND LOUISA ADAMS

1

AMONG the first five Presidents who followed Mr. Washington, Mr. Madison represented a conspicuous exception—he had never been an Ambassador, a Minister Plenipotentiary and Extraordinary, and his lady had never been out of the country. Mr. Madison's two predecessors, on the other hand, had rendered notable services abroad, Mr. Jefferson in France, Mr. and Mrs. John Adams in France and in England; and Mr. Madison's two successors, Mr. Monroe and Mr. John Quincy Adams, with their ladies, were even more closely and extensively identified with the diplomatic enterprises of the nation. With the result that, in the persons of Mrs. Monroe and Mrs. John Quincy Adams, there came consecutively to the President's House two ladies trained in the elegant routine of a cosmopolitan experience, versed in the stately amenities of the most brilliant courts in Europe, accustomed to a style of life and intercourse in the capitals of the Continent, after which the social opportunities of Washington City, as they found it, must inevitably have appeared restricted, however highly the presidency itself might be prized as the crown of a political career, and however grateful to them the return to their native land after prolonged absence.

Elizabeth Kortright was born in New York City, in 1768, the daughter of Captain Lawrence Kortright, of the British Army, and Hannah Aspinwall. Kortright was a solid New York name of long standing, closely allied to the Gouverneurs and a half dozen prominent Colonial families; after the Revolution Captain Kortright decided to remain in New York; Elizabeth was educated there, and presented to society in the brilliant days following the evacuation. She was tall and graceful, and extremely beautiful, noted for her arms and shoulders. She was a reigning belle.

And in February, 1786, she married a young lawyer politician, a Mr. James Monroe from Virginia, who seemed to know everybody. They went to Virginia, and Mr. Monroe was in the Legislature. At other times he took his wife with him on circuit for the courts, even after she had "added a daughter," Eliza, to their society; and Elizabeth enjoyed it all, and took pleasure in the Blue Ridge, as a good adopted Virginian, and did not mind the clumsy travel.

And in 1790 Mr. Monroe was a Senator, a strongly anti-Federalist Senator, and for four years they lived in Philadelphia, in the magnificently gay Philadelphia of Mr. Washington's administration.

And then, in 1794, although Mr. Monroe was a determined opponent of Mr. Washington, the President sent him to France, knowing him to be a firm friend of the French—or, possibly, in order to get him out of the Senate!

2

Elizabeth was not seasick, and enjoyed the trip, but they did not stay very long in France. Mr. Monroe was received with "fraternal hugs" by the French National Convention, at a gala session during which everyone seems to have wept with copious republican joy, and Elizabeth was immediately hailed as "la belle Américaine," and managed to extricate the Marquise de Lafayette from the perils of the Force prison; but Mr. Monroe did not approve of Mr. Jay's treaty with England, and said so very loudly, and in 1796 he was recalled. There followed three years of retirement, after a stormy argument as to why Mr. Monroe should have been sent to France in the first place, whereupon Elizabeth found herself the Governor's Lady of Virginia.

That was in 1799, and in 1801 Mr. Jefferson became President and the Federalists were all biting

their thumbs, and in 1802 Mr. Jefferson sent Mr.
Monroe back to France, to talk to Citizen Talleyrand
about Louisiana, and some other matters. There is
no space in these pages for a discussion of those in-
tricate conversations which resulted in the purchase
by the United States, for a perfectly fabulous sum
as they viewed it, of a vague territory which a great
many citizens were convinced contained nothing but
gigantic savages, vast prairies filled with wild beasts,
and enormous mountains of salt. Nor for any recital
of the heartbreaking, procrastinated, footless negoti-
ations which Mr. Jefferson's opportunist, passion-
ately pacifist policies forced Mr. Monroe to undertake subsequently, at Paris, at London, at Madrid,
and entirely without success. It would be the story of
an honest, painstaking, rather glum and endlessly
unlucky man, obstructed by his colleagues, snubbed
by the English—he and his lady, since Mr. Jefferson
persisted in being, so it seemed to them, unspeak-
ably offensive to Minister Merry and his wife at
Washington—hoodwinked by the French, bamboo-
zled by the Spaniards.

One can only outline—but so incompletely—a picture of Elizabeth tasting the pleasures of that green
and gold Paris of the Consulate and Empire, in which
there were so many bargains in furniture to be made;
that gayest of cities, vivid with uniforms, ablaze with
accumulating glories, resonant with conquering

drums—and the clamor of auction rooms. Travelling with the baby—for another girl, Maria Hester, had been born in 1803—in the great *berline* behind whistling postilions, from the Channel to the frontiers of Spain. Visiting Eliza in her school at St. Germain—the Seminary of the Mountain of Good Air, which that celebrated lady, Madam Campan, had opened in the old Hotel de Rohan, in the beautiful suburb overlooking the Seine.

She was the oldest sister of that Citizen Genêt, who had a while before made such a stir in America, and in the days preceding the Terror she had been one of Queen Marie Antoinette's favorite ladies in waiting, her chosen friend, and one of the last to leave her at the Tuileries on the terrible afternoon of August 10, 1792—so that, at first, she had had trouble with her school as a result of her royalist affiliation. But one day Napoleon sent her his stepdaughter, Hortense Beauharnais, and the school became fashionable; and when Eliza Monroe, and with her the Pinckney girls, came bringing American gold dollars in place of the payments in fuel and provisions which the other pupils had been making, the school began to prosper. And when Elizabeth went there to visit, she found the most select academy for young females in the country, a schoolroom of future queens and duchesses, and her daughter, Eliza, one of the most popular inmates of the establishment, on

terms of the most cordial intimacy with Hortense
and all those other great young ladies of imperial
France.   An intimacy which may possibly have
turned Eliza's head a little; at all events, she was to
cause a great deal of trouble some years later in quite
unimperial Washington.

But the delights of Napoleon's Paris, the pleasures
of collecting furniture and bric à brac, the journey-
ings across France, the visits to stately Madam Campan, came to their unavoidable end.   In 1807, the
Monroes were back in America, and Mr. Monroe was
not pleased with the way he had been treated, and
carried a chip on his shoulder.   But in 1811 he was
again chosen to be Governor of Virginia, and almost
immediately Mr. Madison invited him to be his Secretary of State.   Mr. Monroe was a Virginian, he
was now the first officer in the Cabinet, he must, almost inevitably, become President.   It was unfortunate, therefore, and most untimely, that Elizabeth's
health should have begun to fail to such an extent as to prevent her from assuming the social prom-
inence which Washington might have expected of her
—in spite of Mrs. Madison at the President's House
to outshine her—so that in 1817 Mrs. Smith was
obliged to write that "although they have lived seven
years in Washington, both Mr. and Mrs. Monroe are
perfect strangers, not only to me but all the citizens."

It was unfortunate . . .

ELIZABETH MONROE

From an engraving by Buttre

3

And in the meantime another lady was travelling back and forth across Europe in diplomatic *berlines*.

Louisa Catherine Johnson had been born on February 12, 1775—the second daughter of Joshua Johnson and Catherine Nuth—in London, where her father, a native of Maryland, was in business. But with the outbreak of the Revolution Mr. Johnson found it impossible to remain in England; his sympathies were in Maryland, in the Colonies, where other members of his family were taking an active part in the struggle; he retired with his wife and children to Nantes, in France, and was charged by the Federal Congress with the duty of examining the accounts of American officials in Europe dealing with public funds. After the peace he returned to London, as American Consul, and it was there that Louisa was presented to society, and in his house, which had become the gathering place for all Americans in England, that she met, in 1795, a certain young Mr. John Quincy Adams, whose father was Vice President of the United States.

Now this Mr. John Quincy Adams was a very remarkable young man, who had spent a remarkable boyhood in Europe with his father, and who kept a remarkable diary which might well serve as a history of his times. He had not always kept it so successfully, for in 1778, when he was eleven years old, he wrote from France to his mother, Abigail Adams, his "Honored Mamma," that "My Pappa enjoins it upon me to keep a journal, or diary of the Events that happen to me . . . and although I am convinced of the utility, importance and necessity of this Exercise, yet I have not patience and perseverance enough to do it so Constantly as I thought." But in 1784 he was recording such incidents as that "Mr. Adams dined at the Spanish Ambassador's, Count d'Aranda, an old man seventy years of age who married last year a young woman of twenty—peace be with him!" And in 1794 he was Minister to Holland, having, in his twenties only, attracted Mr. Washington's attention by a series of polemic articles which displayed a mastery of argument and retort, "as well," so Mr. Charles Francis Adams records, "as in that superabounding force of invective which sometimes presses an advantage perhaps beyond the limits of legitimate pursuit."

And in 1795, he was in London for a while on official business, which developed into very pleasant business, for when he returned to Holland, in 1796, he was betrothed to Louisa Johnson. To make up, however, for what he condemned as his idleness and dissipation in London, he did an enormous amount of reading and studying for the remainder of the year. And then, in April, 1797, he was appointed Minister to Portugal. He went to London—and was informed that his father had been elected President of the United States.

The event had not been unexpected. John Quincy had written to tell his mother "that upon the contingency of my father's being placed in the first magistracy, I shall never give him any trouble by solicitation for office of any kind." But Mr. Washington had also written to his successor to tell him that—

"if my wishes would be of any avail, they should go to you in a strong hope that you will not withhold merited promotion from Mr. John Adams because he is your son. For without intending to compliment the father or the mother . . . I give it as my decided opinion that Mr. Adams is the most valuable public character we have abroad."

And so, instead of going to Portugal, John Quincy was to go to Prussia, to make a treaty with King Frederick William II. He went in October, but first, on July 26, 1797—

"At nine this morning I went . . . to Mr. Johnson's, and thence to the Church of the parish of All Hallows, Barking, where I was married to Louisa Catherine Johnson, the second daughter of Joshua and Catherine Johnson. . . . We were married before eleven in the morning, and immediately after went out to see Tilney House, one of the splendid country seats for which this country is distinguished."

4

On November 7, 1797, they arrived in Berlin where they were "questioned at the gates by a dapper lieutenant who did not know . . . who the United States of America were," and taken to the Hotel de Russie. And nine days later King Frederick William II was dead, and succeeded by his son, so that tremendous complications arose concerning John Quincy's credentials, in the midst of which, going "by guess" and relying solely on the "address calendar," they were obliged to make their formal requests for audiences to the proper personages, sending cards to the Dowager Landgrave of Hesse-Cassel, to the Princess Radziwill, to the King's brothers, to one Excellency after another.

It would not have done, in meticulous Prussia, to have ignored anyone, but the visits were all made finally, and the necessary conversational inanities exchanged with the Dowager Landgrave of Hesse-Cassel, and all those other worthies who seemed to "have a few general ideas respecting us which they gather from the newspapers which they all read very assiduously." And then they settled down to it—to the court functions, and receptions, and balls of that somewhat provincial capital; to the opera, where "the scenery was magnificent, the music pretty good, the performers tolerable, the house small and very

badly lighted," and where "no sort of notice was taken
of the King" because the audience was too busy ad-
miring Queen Louise; to the endless games of whist
and reversi with which the members of the diplomatic corps interspersed their official labors; and to
the military reviews which were constantly taking
place at Potsdam.

Two sons were born, in 1799 and in 1801. There
was a summer's journey to Saxony and Bohemia, in
the course of which it became apparent that "the
inns upon these German roads are seldom good."
The rooms were always crowded, sometimes there
was only straw on the floor, and on other occasions
they slept "between sheets not altogether clean." The
beds were all extremely narrow and very short, the
blankets were replaced by suffocating "feather beds,"
and the pillows had a piece of linen "sewed upon one
side . . . and therefore very seldom washed." Another time they spent three months in Silesia, for the
purpose of restoring Louisa's ailing health; but, although she liked it and enjoyed herself there, Berlin,
Prussia in general, did not agree with her—in spite
of many kindnesses from a host of friends—she was
constantly indisposed, and they were not sorry when
in 1801 a forthcoming change of administration at
home caused President Adams to recall them.

They sailed from Hamburg in July and arrived at
Philadelphia on September 4. John Quincy went at

once to Massachusetts, while Louisa took this opportunity to visit her family, now also returned to America, at Frederictown. "I have," John Quincy noted, "parted, for the first time since my marriage, from my wife." Back in Boston, during the following years, it was inevitable that he should take a part in politics. In 1802, he was elected to the Massachusetts Senate on the Federal list; in 1803, they sent him to the Senate of the United States for six years.

A journey of twenty days took the Adamses from Quincy to Washington, where they found room in the home of Louisa's sister, Mrs. Hellen, in whose house a younger sister, Catherine, was also living. There Mr. Adams—one must not call him John Quincy any more— found a mode of life "more uniform." He rose at seven, wrote until nine, breakfasted, dressed; soon after ten he went to the Capitol, walking the two miles in forty-five minutes; the Senate sat until two or three, he was home for dinner at four; the evening was spent "idly" with his older boy, or with the ladies to whom he often read aloud for an hour or two; supper was at nine or ten, and "eleven is the hour for bed." Sometimes they dined out, at a Senator's, at Mr. Jefferson's, whose tall stories did not in the least impress Mr. Adams. Occasionally he took Louisa to the races. In 1804, they all talked a great deal about Miss Patterson and the folly of her marriage to Jerome Bonaparte.

The years passed, rather quietly, very laboriously, not very gaily, perhaps a little bleakly even. Mr. Adams was so methodical, so precise, so ungenial. He turned Republican and made himself heard in the Senate, where in his manner he was "as I always am, miserably defective, but the substance was not without weight." They went less and less into society, and because of certain private financial embarrassments "the privations to which I have found it necessary to recur have been very painful, as they respect my family and in their effects . . . " In the midst of it all, he found time to write quite graceful poems to Louisa, to "the friend of my bosom," on her birthday. In 1807, a third son was born.

And in 1809, quite unexpectedly, Mr. Madison appointed Mr. Adams Minister Plenipotentiary to Russia. Louisa must pack her trunks again, for a long, dismaying journey to that cold, unknown country. . . .

5

Russia!

They arrived at Petersburg on October 23, 1809, after a stormy and much delayed ocean voyage of seventy-five days, and "engaged an apartment of five indifferent chambers" at the Hotel de Londres. They were a large party; Mr. and Mrs. Adams, the baby, Charles Francis,—the two older boys had been left at home,—Miss Catherine Johnson to keep Louisa company, Mr. Adams's nephew, William Smith, as secretary, Martha Godfrey a chambermaid, and a black manservant called Nelson. And of them all, perhaps, this Nelson was to have the best time in Russia; for he eventually became a member of the Russian Church, was baptised, christened and confirmed all at once with tremendous ceremonials, in the presence of an enormous crowd, by a bishop, "or at least a parson with an episcopal mitre and staff," and entered the Imperial household.

As for the others, there was so much to be done— with the exception of Mr. Adams who had been there before as a boy and remembered some of it, so much to learn. The incredible Russian language, the stoves, the hermetically closed double windows, the jingling "drosskys," the snow, the cold, the terrible, black cold, the beverages—"the quas at two kopecks the bottle, and the chitslisky at five; they have a taste of small beer," Mr. Adams found, "with an acid not unpalatable to me, though much so to all the rest of the family." There was the usual wearisome pother of introductions, of formal audiences, of rigid formalities, of ceremonial presentations to the Emperor, Alexander I—a good soul who did not like flannel vests—to the Empress, to the Empress Dowager, to a whole retinue of Grand Dukes and Princes. There were three months of necessary social engagements, an endless round of dinners and balls to be attended and returned, so that in January, 1810, Mr. Adams was hoping that they might promise themselves "for the future a more tranquil life," since until then he had been obliged to record that—

"We rise seldom earlier than nine in the morning— often not before ten. Breakfast. Visits to receive, or visits to make, until three, soon after which the night comes on. At four we dine, and pass the evening either abroad until very late, or at our lodgings with company until ten or eleven o'clock. The night parties abroad seldom break up until four or five o'clock in the morning. It is a life of such irregularity and dissipation as I cannot and will not continue to lead."

For him, with his studious, careful habits, it was irksome; for Louisa, with her continuously impaired health, it was almost out of the question. But a brave attempt had to be made, as often as possible, so as not to give offence. Court balls that cost eighteen thousand roubles and consumed fifteen thousand wax candles, where the Emperor sought out Louisa on purpose to dance a Polonaise with her; endless church festivals and Te Deums, at which the wish for Napoleons's downfall was father to the prayer; recurring ceremonies, birthdays, launchings, civic fêtes; Easter with its eggs of glass, and marble, and gilt wood to be exchanged with everyone; May Day, and the procession of carriages, with postilions and teams of four, and six, and even eight gaily caparisoned horses; sleighing parties and ice carnivals; visits to schools, to factories, to charitable institutions; soirees at the theatre, at the opera, at the Imperial drawing room; dinners, dinners, dinners—there was no end to it, in the brilliant, snow spangled, bell ringing, diamond and fur bedizened city of the Emperor of all the Russias.

And a house to be chosen, and put in order, and managed. And if it was not on the scale of Mr. de Caulaincourt, the French Ambassador's establishment—which cost a million roubles a year, required the services of sixty-five persons, and sheltered fifty-six horses in its stables—still it was very expensive and complicated.

"We have a maitre d'hotel or steward," Mr. Adams complained; "a cook who has under him two scullions—mujiks; a Swiss, or porter; two footmen; a mujik to make the fires; a coachman and postilion . . . a femme de chambre of Mrs. Adams, who is the wife of the steward, a housemaid and a laundry maid. The Swiss, the cook and one of the footmen are married and their wives all live in the house. The steward has two children and the washerwoman a daughter, all of whom are kept in the house. . . . The firewood is luckily included as part of the rent. On all . . . articles of consumption the cook and steward first make their profits. . . and next make free pillage of the articles themselves. The steward takes the same liberty with my wines."

It was a good deal to ask of New England frugality, this happy-go-lucky Muscovite house party!

But when all was said and done, it was lonely in Petersburg. Only one other Minister had his lady with him, although if local gossip could be believed, as indeed it was, some of the bachelor Ambassadors were not entirely destitute of feminine consolation. Mr. de Caulaincourt, for instance, everyone knew why he had his house on the Peterhof Road; because Madame Vlodek—but no matter—it was lonely in Petersburg for Louisa. She lived there for five years "as a stranger to all but the kind regards of the Imperial family, and I quitted its gaudy loneliness without a sigh." There were two children at home; a little girl born in 1811 died within the year; America was a long way off and news travelled slowly; Mr. Adams did not mind the cold, but for Louisa it was a misery —this "sterile heartlessness of a Russian residence of icy coldness"—and she was perhaps never quite well. The only "alloy" in Mr. Adams's "felicity" arose from "the delicacy of my wife's constitution, the ill health which has afflicted her much of the time, and the misfortunes she has suffered from it."

And they quarrelled a little. "Our union has not been without its trials," Mr. Adams admitted, "nor

invariably without dissensions between us. There
are many differences of sentiment, of tastes and of
opinions in regard to domestic economy and to the
education of children between us." She was probably
much more tolerant, much more liberal. "There are
natural frailties of temper in both of us; both being
quick and irascible, and mine being sometimes harsh."
But she had always been "a faithful and affectionate
wife, and a careful, tender, indulgent and watchful
mother." He might have added that she had also been
a gracious hostess when illness did not prevent,
a spirited, courageous lady, a good traveller who bore
the discomforts and vicissitudes of the long roads
with fortitude.

At all events, she was to have a conspicuous opportunity to display these qualities. For in 1814, Mr.
Adams went to Ghent, to assist at the making of the
treaty of peace with England; Louisa remained
alone in Russia—her personal household had returned
one by one to America—for another dreary winter;
and in 1815 she found herself summoned across Europe to join him at Paris.

6

It was a disorganized, devastated, precarious
Europe, filled with disorderly, vagrant soldiery. The
Allies had taken Paris, Napoleon was on the Island

of Elba, the Bourbon Louis XVIII was back on the throne of France. It was supposed that peace had come. Louisa was very much alarmed at the prospect of her journey, and worried about the sale of her furniture which Mr. Adams had recommended. One wonders if Louisa was not just a little afraid, often, of Mr. Adams, a little restive under his strictly economical accountings, a little apprehensive of his critical Adams nature.

"Conceive the astonishment your letter caused me if you can," she wrote. "I know not what to do about the selling of the goods and I fear I shall be much imposed upon. This is a heavy trial but I must get through it at all risks, and if you receive me with the conviction that I have done my best I shall be amply rewarded. I am in so much confusion that it is hardly possible for me to write you."

She left Petersburg on the afternoon of February 12, 1815, in a Russian coach on runners, with her seven-year-old boy—for whom a bed had been arranged in the front of the carriage—accompanied by a French nurse who had come to her that very day, and two menservants, one of whom, Baptiste, had been a prisoner of war in Mitau. And at first, matters went smoothly enough; she was paid every attention, and elaborately entertained at Riga by the Governor; but it was bitterly cold, so that during one

stage "our provisions were all hard frozen . . . and
even the madeira wine had become solid ice."

They exchanged the runners for wheels and went
on into Courland, where—

"once or twice the carriage sank so deep in the snow
. . . that we had to ring up the inhabitants . . . to
dig us out. For this purpose the bells appeared to
be commonly used and our postilion appealed to them
without hesitation, and the signal was immediately
understood."

Then, at Mitau, an alarming thing happened. Louisa
had refused the invitation of her friend, Countess
Mengs, and had determined to proceed to the next
post house, when the innkeeper approached her with
great mystery and caution, informed her of a frightful murder which had taken place on that road the
night before, and warned her that her servant, Baptiste, was a notorious character in Mitau, and a vil-
lain of the deepest dye. But Louisa replied that she
was under bond to take him to France unless he behaved improperly, that the carriage was ordered, and
that she was going—"from a proud and foolhardy
spirit," as she afterwards admitted.

They started off, "under the most uneasy impres-
sions," and four miles out the postilion announced
that he was lost. Until nearly midnight they were
"jolted over hills, through swamps and holes, and into

valleys into which no carriage had surely ever passed before, and my whole heart was filled with unspeakable terrors for the safety of the child;" and then the horses were worn out and Baptiste had to be sent on alone to see what he could find. In the coach, they waited, under the wintry midnight sky, on the slope of a lost hill in Courland, while the child slept "sweetly" in his little improvised bed. But Baptiste found a house, and they were taken in for the night.

The Vistula was crossed, on thin, perilous ice, with men in front sounding with poles, and after a while they were in Prussia—trundling through a gloomy, frozen countryside, filled with the "fearful remnants of man's fury." And the nearer they approached to Berlin, the more impertinent Baptiste became, until Louisa threatened him with dismissal, after which he was more respectful, but "there was something threatening in his look that did not please me, but I was afraid to notice it." They went on and on—encountering minor vicissitudes, broken wheels, enforced lodgings in chance roadside dens—and Louisa kept her money bags hidden, letting the men think that she only drew enough at each town for the next stretch.

Berlin was a haven of refuge, a joy, a resuscitation of "pleasant recollections of the past, and youth seemed again to be decked with rosy smiles." They stayed a week, and Louisa made her presence known

to some of her old acquaintances of fourteen years
before, and was received with affectionate delight and
with the friendliest courtesies. She felt at home in
Berlin—but Mr. Adams was waiting, and they must
go. Through Prussia, across the German States,
running everywhere into groups of disbanded soldiers, so that Louisa found it advisable after dark, in
order to escape annoyance and insult, to make a pre-
tense of military identity by putting on her little boy's
toy soldier hat with the big plume, and showing his
sword at the window. And at Eisenach there was a
rumor that Napoleon was again in France, and at
Hanau it was confirmed.

They went on, hearing nothing on all sides but
praise for the French and their bravery, and curses
for the Allies and "the far renowned horrors and
cruelties of the ruffian Cossacks." And in Frankfort
the two menservants refused to go any further, because there would now be conscription in France, and
Louisa was obliged to proceed along circuitous routes
—so as to avoid the troops which were being reas-
sembled—with only a young Prussian lad of fourteen
as courier. They passed through Baden, where everyone was certain that Napoleon had been captured and
shot; they were delayed by "wagons of every description full of soldiers . . . rushing towards the
frontier, roaring national songs and apparently in
great glee at the idea of a renewal of hostilities;"

and finally they were at Strasbourg—in which Louisa, for some unaccountable reason, managed to find a resemblance to Worcester, Massachusetts.

She was very tired and ill, but there were passports to be seen to, and a new servant, Dupin, to be engaged—and they were off again, through a France seething with troops, roaring for Napoleon, damning the Cossacks. All went well until beyond Epernay, and then suddenly there was an uproar on the road, a cursing and shouting that they were Russians —because of the Petersburg coach—a threatening of swords and bayonets. Louisa had driven right in to the midst of Napoleon's Imperial Guard, on its way to meet the Emperor. She explained that they were Americans—loud cheers—she waved her handkerchief, she cried "Vive l'Empereur!" and *vive* anything else which the soldiers seemed to require. They let her go. With the general in command and his staff escorting her carriage, they cut through the entire column, at the mercy of this utterly undisciplined and very considerably intoxicated rabble, which was so soon, at Waterloo, to pass into immortality. Poor little Charles Francis was terrified, and sat like a white marble statue.

And the night at the inn was a long terror, with the coach hidden away, and stragglers pounding at the doors all through the sleepless hours. But the next morning the road was clear and they went on, to be met with the news that forty thousand men were around Paris and that a battle was imminent.

"This news startled me very much," Louisa confessed, "but on cool reflection I thought it best to persevere. I was travelling at great expense, a thing quite unsuited to the paltry salary of an American Minister, and I was sure that if there was any danger Mr. Adams would have come to meet me. . . . "

But Mr. Adams was in Paris, going to the theatre, and to the opera, and waiting with the crowds to see Napoleon come in, and Louisa had to finish her journey alone. And because she was the only private traveller on the roads, and because she had six horses to her coach, they began to say that she was Napoleon's niece, Stephanie—and Dupin, most discreet of couriers, smiled a little and did not deny it. And at eleven o'clock on the evening of March 23, they rolled into the courtyard of the Hotel du Nord, in Paris, and Mr. Adams was enormously surprised to hear of all these alarms and perils. The city had been so quiet, it had never occurred to him—never, apparently, struck him that a lady travelling alone through France in those parlous days might be subjected to the most dire inconveniences. He had been expecting her, and he had come home from the play that evening and been annoyed at not finding her there. He was in his rooms when she arrived.

The conviction grows that Mr. Adams was not a pleasant person. . . .

7

But Paris was splendid, although it rained a great deal that spring. The royal family had decamped during the night of March 19, after issuing warlike proclamations which no one showed the slightest inclination to observe. The people had gone around, instead, tearing down Bourbon emblems, and learning again to shout "Vive l'Empereur!" which made more noise, somehow, than "Vive le Roi!" The Emperor himself had arrived at about nine o'clock on the evening of March 20, at the head of the army which had been sent out to oppose him—making his way through roaring crowds, gaily feeding the fugitive King's manifestoes to triumphant bonfires, into the courtyard of the Tuileries where they had dragged him from his carriage and borne him shoulder high up the staircase, led by that same Mr. de Caulaincourt who had been at Petersburg. In the streets they were selling tricolor cockades, "the cockade that doesn't get dirty!" In the audience chamber, Eliza Monroe's old schoolmate, Hortense, was busy on her hands and knees ripping off the royalist symbols sewed onto the carpet, and revealing the old Bonaparte emblems underneath. Everywhere, the Lilies had faded, the Violets were blooming.

There followed that brilliant twilight of the Napoleonic gods, the last trooping of the Eagles, the swarming of the Golden Bees, the Hundred Days that were to end at Waterloo. All Paris pushed up and down the boulevards, jammed its way into the Tuileries to see the Little Corporal, surged in and out of the Place du Carrousel to watch the troops pass by in review. In the evening one went to the theatre to sing popular songs and listen to plays filled with patriotic allusions; one sat in the gardens of the Palais Royal and admired the old uniforms of Iéna and Austerlitz.

Louisa saw it all; she went to the theatre, and heard them cheer the little man with the cocked hat when he came into his box; she went to dinners and balls; she visited General Lafayette; she had a good time, a holiday time under spring skies, after the cold Russian years. Even Mr. Adams found that "the tendency to dissipation . . . seems to be irresistible." And then, on May 16, they had to go, because Mr. Adams was named Minister to England.

London, Louisa's native city, after an absence of eighteen years. But it was a very different London, filled with strangers, revisited under trying circumstances; for Mr. and Mrs. John Quincy Adams were there representing America at the close of an armed dispute between the two countries, just as once before Mr. and Mrs. John Adams had come bringing

THE ENTRY OF NAPOLEON INTO PARIS FROM ELBA IN 1815

From a contemporary American print

credentials from the newly emancipated Colonies. It had not been pleasant then, it was not to be much more so now, and there were many incidents in store to remind Mr. Adams "how small a place my person or my station occupies in the notice of these persons." That extremely public character, the Duke of Wellington, for instance, could never get it through his head just what it was that Mr. Adams was doing in London, although when they met he seemed to recollect having seen him somewhere before.

But for Louisa, when she was not indisposed, the time passed not too disagreeably. They took a house in the suburbs, at Ealing, and the two older boys came over from America to join their mother. Mr. and Mrs. Adams drove into town occasionally to attend a function at the palace; to see the Waterloo illuminations, which were "very few and very bad;" to push their way through the mobs at the Lord Mayor's ball, where it was impossible for more than five couples to dance at once, and where—

"the heat was scarcely less oppressive, several ladies fainted, and the Lady Mayoress sat in state with her smelling bottle constantly at her nostrils to keep herself from fainting. . . . The dinner tables were yet standing and covered with people standing on them. We were obliged to pass over them to get out of the hall."

They were not at all sorry when, in April, 1817, they received word from Washington that President Monroe had chosen Mr. Adams to be his Secretary of State. They sailed from Cowes, on June 15, and landed at New York on August 6. They had been gone from America just eight years and a day.

8

And now these two ambassadresses, Mrs. Monroe and Mrs. Adams, were together in Washington, in the two most conspicuous social positions in the land, for all the world to see. But the trouble was, as far as Mrs. Monroe, at least, was concerned, that the world did not see her.

"People seem to think," Mrs. Smith wrote in November, 1817, "we shall have great changes in social intercourse and customs. Mr. and Mrs. Monroe's manners will give a tone to all the rest. Few persons are admitted to the great house, and not a single lady has yet seen Mrs. Monroe, Mrs. Cutts excepted. . . . She is always at home to Mrs. Cutts."

Now this was most provoking; for if not a single lady, the fortunate Mrs. Cutts excepted, had seen Mrs. Monroe, then not a single lady either had viewed the restored magnificences of Mrs. Monroe's apartments, which was perhaps even more important. For there was a new President's House, at last, to replace the one burned by the British in 1814, containing one thousand two hundred and ninety panes of glass and twenty-six marble chimney pieces—so it was said—and in Mrs. Hay's rooms, for Eliza Monroe was married now, there were eleven armchairs, a settee and a crown bed draped with cambric adorned with a red and yellow fringe. In other words, Washington was bursting with curiosity to see the splendors with which Mr. Monroe had invested the presidential residence.

For it was all Mr. Monroe's doing. Mr. Monroe had a very pretty taste in bric à brac, and he had brought over with him from France a considerable quantity of extremely elegant furniture—including two hundred and eighty-six pieces of white and gold china—which he had sold to the Commissioner of Public Buildings. But that was not enough, and Congress had appropriated twenty thousand dollars for further embellishment which Mr. Monroe had ordered from Russell and Lafarge in France. At the same time, Mr. Monroe had employed a great number of local artisans, hewers of wood and workers in damask, who thought nothing of sending in bills amounting to four hundred dollars for a pair of curtains with trimmings. As for the new furniture from France, Mr. Monroe knew exactly what he wanted —with "a mingled regard . . . to the simplicity and purity of our institutions" and to the character of the People represented in the building—and he had made the most careful estimates, for he was a connoisseur.

But unhappily Russell and Lafarge had not kept within the estimates. For the Oval Room, for instance, they had changed the mahogany to gilt wood, with crimson silk trimmings and fringes, since, as Mr. Monroe should have known, "mahogany is not generally admitted in the furniture of a saloon, even at private gentlemen's houses." They had had trouble, too, with the ornamental clocks, as it had been difficult to "secure pendules without nudities," and there were, of course, to be no nudities at the White House. This was unfortunate, as was the fact that the Commissioner of Public Buildings eventually absconded with some twenty thousand dollars of the public funds, leaving Mr. Monroe himself at some pains to clarify his innocent share in these dubious proceedings.

But in the meantime the furniture had arrived, along with "thirty-nine cases containing twelve hundred bottles Champagne and Burgundy wine . . . and seven cases of which six are for Mrs. Monroe . . . and one for Mrs. Decatur." And Washington wanted very much to see these treasures of Mr. Monroe's selection, and finally on New Year's Day, 1818, the public curiosity was gratified. And Mr. Monroe had really done it very handsomely. There was a gilt bronze chandelier with crystals, for fifty lights; there were canapés nine feet long, and tabourets, bergères and gondolas; there were vases, and mirrors, and clocks without end; there were gold and rose hangings; there was a piano from Erard; there were thirty-six egg cups and twelve dozen dinner plates; there was a gilt bronze dining room centerpiece of seven items, with baskets, and mirrors, and pedestals, all covered with garlands and vines, and figures of Bacchus—which seem inappropriate, somehow, in retrospect—and which occupied a space thirteen feet long and brought the manufacturer a net loss of two thousand francs; there was a great deal of everything. And on top of that Congress appropriated another thirty thousand dollars for carpets, table linen and cut glass—including two dozen champagne glasses.

Washington hoped that Mrs. Monroe would entertain a great deal. . . .

9

But the trouble was, again, that Mrs. Monroe did not entertain. She was too constantly indisposed— if not seriously ill—and her daughter, Mrs. Hay, who quite obviously ruled the White House and everyone in it, including Mr. Monroe, did not allow her mother to exert herself. Mrs. Monroe presided at an occasional White House dinner—rather gloomy functions in the French style, with a cloud of servants actually handing the dishes around—and she held her weekly

Wednesday drawing rooms—drearily formal, somewhat European affairs, crowded with—

"secretaries, senators, foreign ministers, consuls, audi-
tors, accountants, officers . . . farmers, merchants,
parsons, priests, lawyers, judges, auctioneers and
nothingarians—all with their wives and some with
their gawky offspring . . . some in shoes, most in
boots and many in spurs; some snuffing, others chew-
ing . . . some with powdered heads, others frizzled
and oiled."

But except for these official hospitalities, Mrs. Monroe did not mingle with society, or permit society to
mingle with her.

It was sensible enough, under the circumstances.
Mrs. Madison, to be sure, had visited everyone, but
her health had been seriously impaired in consequence; Washington had grown considerably, and
was always full of transients; Mrs. Adams herself
was only giving weekly teas and returning visits,
making none on her own initiative to newly arrived
ladies or to Senatorial and Congressional families.
And if Mrs. Adams was not equal to the task, Mrs.
Monroe was still less able to attempt the social routine of her predecessor, and she therefore determined
neither to make visits nor to return any, leaving this
duty to her daughter. But unfortunately, again, Mrs.
Hay did not pay all the visits which Washington ex-

pected of her; she would not call on any of the ladies of the diplomatic corps, because these had not called on her in the first place; she apparently influenced her father to keep all the foreign Ministers "at a cold and cautious distance;" she injected the jealousies and vengeances of her private feuds into the domestic councils of the White House, and colored all its relations with society—so that, in a very few months, Washington was in a turmoil of dissension and recrimination.

It was the era of good feeling in politics; it could easily have been one of cordiality in society, in spite of the foreign tendencies exhibited by the two ex-ambassadresses, and in spite of the indispositions which continually beset them and served to emphasize their natural aloofness and reserve. Mrs. Adams was a person of great charm and tact, endowed with the highest mental qualities. Mrs. Monroe was beautiful, elegant and accomplished; they were both eminently competent to offset the less congenial external aspects and manners of their otherwise extremely worthy husbands. But Eliza Hay would have none of it. She had sat on the same school bench with duchesses and queens, she was the President's daughter and the undisputed mistress of his establishment, she was an obstinate little firebrand, whom Mr. Adams considered one of the principal causes of the "senseless war" which agitated the community, and she was

determined to have her pound of etiquette, even at
the cost of her parents' popularity, and the peace of
mind of the entire Cabinet. For while Mr. Adams,
for instance, should have been let alone to discuss the
Floridas and other delicate international subjects, he
found himself perpetually being interrupted to render
decisions in that weighty matter of the "etiquette visiting" which was become "an affair of state," and a
question of "high importance."

It began right away, in January, 1818. Mrs. Monroe sent for Mrs. Adams to tell her that "the ladies
had taken offense at her for not paying them the first
visit." All the ladies—transient ladies and resident
ladies of Congress. And then the diplomatic corps
took a hand. Mr. de Neuville, the French Minister,
gave a ball and wished Mr. and Mrs. Monroe to attend. Mr. Monroe replied that it was contrary to
precedent, and Mrs. Monroe refused to go anywhere
without her husband. It was finally decided that
Mrs. Hay should go—but that lady wished it dis-
tinctly understood that her presence was not official,
and did not in any way alter her decision not to visit
any of the Ministers' wives. And since foreign en-
voys were involved, Mr. Adams, Secretary of State,
was called in to carry these infinitely petty messages.

The affair went on. Mr. Monroe got into trouble
with his diplomatic dinners. It had always been customary to invite the Secretary of State with the Min-

isters, and since none of them were Ambassadors of the First Rank the Secretary took precedence. But now the other secretaries demanded that they be included, and on an equal footing with Mr. and Mrs. Adams. But the Ministers had no intention of seeing themselves, and their wives, superseded by the entire Cabinet. In the capital of the Republic, in that shrine of all the democratic virtues—the White House in which Mr. Jefferson had once sent his guests in to dinner *pele mele* and *en masse*—the matter of aristocratic precedence suddenly became of vital concern. Washington was beginning to take itself frightfully seriously. Mr. Monroe tried inviting the Ministers without any secretaries, and with only "some respectable private citizens." But the Ministers did not care to dine with respectable private citizens. They wanted secretaries, but in their proper place. They were finally given Mr. Adams, and one other secretary in rotation.

And the affair went on. In December, 1819, the ladies of Washington were boycotting Mrs. Monroe, so that one of her drawing rooms opened "to a beggarly row of empty chairs. Only five females attended, three of whom were foreigners." Mrs. Adams was scarcely faring any better, and at one large invited party prepared at her house only three ladies condescended to appear. The long and the short of it was that the Senators expected to be visited by

Mrs. Adams, and her failure to comply was causing "uneasiness, heartburnings, and severe criticism." Mr. Monroe called a Cabinet meeting. They sat for two hours and finally decided to continue doing each as his wife saw fit with regard to this "paltry passion for precedence." On the other hand, Mr. Adams was to prepare for the President a statement of his attitude and that of Mrs. Adams.

Mr. Adams had many better things to do, but, for so accomplished a pamphleteer as he was, the occasion was not without certain compensating opportunities. Mrs. Adams, he informed Mr. Monroe, visited no lady as a stranger in order to avoid invidious distinctions. As for the Senate, Mr. Adams had the highest regard for the Senate, having himself been a Senator. But he had never been called upon by department heads. It seemed to him that to pay visits of ceremony to Congress at every session "would not only be a very useless waste of time, but not very compatible with the discharge of the real and important duties of the departments," nor did the custom appear "altogether congenial to the republican simplicity of our institutions." To the President of the Senate Mr. Adams then wrote that it was his impression that the Government was "a government for the transaction of business." Concerning Mrs. Adams, she had always invited without formality any lady who cared to come to her house, and she had "only regretted the more rigorous etiquette of those who have declined inasmuch as it bereft her of the happiness which she would have derived from a more successful cultivation of their acquaintance."

Yes. There was a little less talk in the Senate about visits after that—but Mrs. Hay was still at it, and in March, 1820, when her sister, Maria Hester, was married at the White House to her cousin, Samuel Gouverneur, Mrs. Hay informed the diplomatic corps that they were not expected to take any notice of the event; a suggestion which the diplomatic corps followed with considerable alacrity. . . .

10

But the years were passing. Mr. Monroe went into his second term, and seemed, at least to Mr. S. G. Goodrich, dull, sleepy and personally insignificant. His dress was black and rusty, his neckcloth small, ropy and carelessly tied, his frill matted, his countenance wilted with age, study and care. Altogether, he appeared "owlish and ordinary." Mrs. Monroe was almost always ill. They can neither of them have been very happy in the gaudy White House.

Outside, in the town, Mr. Adams's friends were urging him to mingle more in society, until he complained that "dinners, evening parties and balls have absorbed an unreasonable portion of my time," but he indulged himself in order to "repel the reproach . . .

of a reserved, gloomy, unsocial temper." And his friends were urging Mrs. Adams to influence him to a greater geniality, to a less fastidious reserve; he seemed to disdain any champion but himself, and "now my dear Madam, all this won't do"—because it was 1823, and Mr. Adams was a candidate for the presidency, whether he wished it or not. It was a very bitter, vicious campaign in which a dozen journals were "pouring forth continual streams of slander" upon his character, and in which it seemed "as if every liar and calumniator in the country was at work day and night" to destroy his reputation. And Louisa must have encouraged him, and kept him in humor, and in 1824 she did a very gracious thing which helped him—she gave a ball in honor of a dangerous rival, General Andrew Jackson.

> "Wend you with the world tonight?
> Brown and fair, and wise and witty,
> Eyes that float in seas of light,
> Laughing mouths and dimples pretty,
> Belles and matrons, maids and madams,
> All are gone to Mrs. Adams' . . ."

It was the talk of the town. They hung the ball room with garlands and tissue paper, and festooned the pillars with laurel, and chalked the floor with eagles and patriotic mottoes. A thousand people came. And on February 9, 1825, Mr. Adams was elected. They went to the White House to pay their respects to Mrs. Monroe at her last drawing room, and saw her, gracious and regal, her dress a "superb black velvet, neck and arms bare and beautifully formed, her hair in puffs and dressed high on the head, and ornamented with white ostrich plumes; round her neck an elegant pearl necklace." All the rooms were in use with great hickory wood fires in the open fireplaces, and wine was passed around on silver salvers by colored waiters in livery. General Jackson was there too, and Mr. Adams was very rude to him, without ever suspecting it. Mr. Adams was not a good mixer, nor a graceful winner. In the late evening, a band of musicians came and serenaded him at his house, which probably surprised him. . . .

11

Inauguration Day came around. Mrs. Adams gave a big reception; they visited Mr. Monroe; they attended the ball at Carusi's—and they returned, at eleven o'clock, to their own home, for Mrs. Monroe was too sick to leave the President's House, and it was not until some time later that the Adamses were able to take possession. As for the Monroes, they retired to Oak Hill, in Loudoun County, Virginia—to an existence increasingly beset with financial cares—and there, in 1830, Mrs. Monroe died.

At the White House, there followed four years conspicuous primarily for the rigidity of their routine. Mr. Adams arose very early, at five in summer; he took a walk or else, in season, bathed in the Potomac, an enthusiastic, if elderly, Triton; before breakfast he studied the Scriptures for a while; at the close of the day's official duties he dined, passed an hour or so with Mrs. Adams, and then was busy at his writing until eleven. An amazingly industrious man, a voracious reader, a composer of poetry, an author of monographs—to say nothing of the stupendous diary—who would have preferred to have devoted his entire life to the pursuit of literature. He enjoyed gardening, billiards, and horseback riding. He was —because of his uncanny facility for giving offense, his inability to appear conciliating and gracious— enormously unpopular.

He abstained from all private functions in society, and found his own levees "more and more insupportable." Mrs. Adams held them once a week, and later once a fortnight—evening receptions at which refreshments were handed around, which was an innovation, and which were crowded by curiosity seekers from every walk of life. Besides the drawing rooms, there was usually a large, weekly dinner, and more rarely a smaller company for the evening. Otherwise, Mrs. Adams received very little and went seldom into society. She kept silkworms, several hundreds of them; she derived keen enjoyment from music and books; she was an extremely retiring, scholarly person. She was also, and ever increasingly, in extremely delicate health. In 1828, Mr. Adams was passing "from one to two hours after dinner with my wife in her chamber, to which she is almost entirely confined by ill health." When she did go out into the world, it was usually to visit her close friend, Mrs. Edward Livingston, the mother of the celebrated Cora, in whose salon Washington contrived to forget even the animosities of the etiquette war. There were domestic events. General Lafayette was entertained. John, the second son, was married to his cousin, Mary Hellen—an arrogant young man who got his nose pulled in the rotunda of the Capitol for having been astonishingly rude to one of General Jackson's supporters. George, the oldest son, died, in 1829—and John himself was not to survive his parents.

It was a formal, frigid, and one suspects—in spite of the colorful crowds at the drawing rooms—rather drab, arduous time at the White House. In contemporary estimation, the Adamses were notorious for a "silent, repulsive, haughty reserve." Beyond the confines of the presidential mansion, things were happening. Mr. Clay was Secretary of State, and wondering how soon he would be President. Mr. Webster was very much in the public ear. Vice President Calhoun was sitting in the Senate—and sitting silently, to his chagrin—listening to that terrible,

vitriolic Mr. John Randolph address him in his spind-
ly voice as "Mr. Speaker! I mean, Mr. President of
the Senate and would-be President of the United
States, which God in His infinite mercy avert!" While
the ladies of Washington were attending evening
parties—and watching their husbands gamble at
whist, and dancing quadrilles, cheats and reels at the
Assemblies in white India crepe dresses trimmed
with flounces—a great many gentlemen wearing blue
or green Bolivar frock coats, and several superim-
posed waistcoats, and large Cossack trousers tucked
into Hessian boots adorned with gold tassels, were
jingling their watchfobs and conducting a presidential campaign even more vicious than the previous
one.

And the outcome of it was that in 1828 General
Jackson was elected.

"You ask how the administration folks look since
their defeat," Mrs. Smith wrote in December.
"They all with one consent . . . appear cheerful and good humored, mix freely and frankly with
the triumphant party. . . . Mr. and Mrs. Adams
have gone a little too far in this assumed gaiety; at
the last drawing room they laid aside the manners
which until now they have always worn, and came
out in a brilliant masquerade dress of social, gay,
frank, cordial manners. . . . The great audience
chamber, never before opened, and now not finished,
was thrown open for dancing, a thing unheard of

LOUISA ADAMS

From an engraving by Storm

before at a drawing room. . . . All the folks attached to the administration made a point of being there. The ladies of the Cabinet in their best bibs and tuckers, most of them in new dresses just arrived from Paris."

And then General Jackson arrived, in his best bib and tucker, and refused to call on Mr. Adams, and on March 3, 1829, the Adamses evacuated the White House and withdrew to Meridian Hill. The ambassadorial régime was at an end.

12

Mr. Adams was sixty-two years old. One might have expected—perhaps Louisa Adams did expect—that he would now be contented to retire from his phenomenal career of public service. But not at all. Some of Mr. Adams's most laborious years, some of his greatest triumphs, still lay before him. In November, 1830, he was chosen to represent his native state in the national House of Representatives. For eighteen years, with his sharp acrimonious tongue, and that "terrible yarring tone in his voice," he made himself more and more conspicuous as the champion of anti-slavery, and at the end, in 1848, it was from his chair in the House that they took him, stricken and unconscious, to his deathbed. It was an innovation, an ex-President in Congress, and there were many who thought it an unbecoming anti-climax. His own family were not any too pleased. But Mr. Adams was delighted; the election had come spontaneously from his own state after a defeat at the national polls; his elevation to the presidency had not been "half so gratifying" to his "inmost soul;" no office conferred upon him had ever given him so much pleasure.

And so, for Mrs. Adams, the endless round went on, Quincy and Boston in the summer, Washington in the winter. But for her they were very quiet years, remote from the fashionable turmoil of society, spent in the company of a few old friends with her books, and her poetry, and her music. For if her husband's tastes were artistic and literary—he wrote and published a whole long poem, *Dermot McMorrogh*, during those years—Louisa's were no less so. She possessed a facile gift of composition in prose and verse, she was capable of excellent translation from the French, she sang, and played charmingly on the pianoforte. They would both have been much happier all their lives in a mode of existence less public, less extravagant of time and energy, in which their talents might have found a greater freedom of expression, a more ample opportunity of fruition. It was the irony of her life, that, called upon to fill conspicuous positions in European and American society, Louisa Adams was not in the least worldly.

The years passed. "I frequent no society," Mr. Adams once wrote, "and with the exception of my daily walks we are confined within the walls of our house as if it were a ship at sea." Once a year, at New Year's, the crowds came pouring into Mrs. Adams's parlor, and once a year Mr. Adams went to pay his respects to the venerable Mrs. Madison. He died on February 23, 1848, and Mrs. Madison a year later.

"It has pleased the Almighty in his perfect wisdom to teach me this sad lesson," Louisa wrote to her sister, Mrs. Boyd, in a letter hitherto unpublished, "for so long repining at our continued perseverance in Public life; which I began to think almost a calamity, in consequence of the creeping infirmities of age which were evidently unfitting us for the fatigues and anxieties attendant upon Public duties and the irregular habits which it necessarily produces. I lived in constant apprehensions of its ill effects, and alas my fears have been too fully realized. But the idea of quitting public life as long as he had the power of acting and the mind to sustain him was so fixed, it only worried him to suggest the wish, and he would constantly answer 'that he should die the moment he gave it up.'

"You may conceive the dreadful shock which I sustained when sent for to the Capitol under the impression that he had only fainted, when I arrived there and found him speechless and dying and without a moment of returning sense to show that he knew that I was near him, and thus he lay until he drew his last breath without a sign of recognition of any of his family. Surrounded by men in the Speaker's room at the Capitol he died at 20 minutes after seven o'clock and I was *forced* to leave him ere the last sign had quivered on his lips; it being necessary they said for the women to go away, 'that the last duties might be performed.'

"Dear Harriet they tell me that it was the act of the Almighty . . . but O can anything compensate for the agony of this last sad parting on Earth, after fifty years of union; without even the privilege of indulging the feelings which all hold sacred at such moments. My senses almost gave way and it seemed as if I had become callous to suffering while my heart seemed breaking. . . . Amid your many sorrows you at least had the blessing of closing your Husband's eyes and receiving his last parting look and hearing his last parting word and the satisfaction of knowing that your life had been devoted to him through weal and woe, to promote his happiness and comfort to the last hour of his existence. This last blessing was denied to me, and I fear I had indulged presumptuous hopes which blinded me to his real situation. . . .

"God bless you my beloved Sister. O how I wish I could visit you, but I am 73 and I cannot hope it. Perhaps you could come to see me at Quincy, that would indeed be a gratification unspeakable; do try. . . ."

Mr. Jefferson, Mr. John Adams and Abigail, Mr. Madison, James and Elizabeth Monroe—they were all at rest. Louisa Adams followed them very soon, on May 15, 1852, at Quincy. And now they were all gone, those colleagues, those successors, those intimates of the Revolutionary and early Federal group. There were new names, new faces, new manners everywhere, a new heaven and a new earth. . . .

Rachel Jackson

NOTE

Shortly after the appearance in magazine form of the informal biography of Rachel Jackson, now reprinted in this volume, the editors of the magazine forwarded to Mr. Minnigerode's publishers a telegram from Nashville, Tennessee, reading in part as follows—

"The people of this section are surprised and indignant at the publication . . . of the article by Meade Minnigerode. They were not prepared to see so unfair and inaccurate a review of such historical personages as President of the United States and his wife, and one permeated with such contemptuous and narrow prejudices as characterized the author, appear in the columns of your great journal. Such a publication is an affront to the truth of history and to that justice at its bar which Tennessee holds to be due the memory of the distinguished man and woman. . . . A public meeting of protest will be held in this city tomorrow. E. B. Stahlman, publisher *The Banner*, Nashville, Tennessee."

On May 21, 1925, the Nashville *Tennessean* printed an account, here reproduced in part, of the aforementioned mass meeting.

"The branding of Meade Minnigerode, author of
'An Informal Biography of Rachel Jackson' . . .
by prominent Tennessee men and women as a 'coward, liar, cur and rascal' . . . and the adoption
of resolutions condemning the article and its author,
featured a public meeting at the Hermitage hotel
at 3:30 P. M., Wednesday. Indignation of Ten-
nesseans at the slurs cast upon their beloved President and war hero and his wife in Mr. Minnigerode's
article . . . burst into flame at the meeting. Leading men and women of the State denounced the
writer of the article in no uncertain terms and
even went so far as to say if all other measures
failed to bring retraction they would like to 'settle the matter of slanders cast upon Rachel Jackson as Andrew Jackson himself settled them with
Dickinson.'

" 'The old pistol which Jackson used on that
memorable occasion still is preserved, and I for one
would be glad to use it again to protect the honor of
our beloved Rachel Jackson, the gracious wife of one
of the greatest statesmen the world has ever known,'
declared Mr. Moore"—the State Librarian and
Archivist of Tennessee— "crystallizing the aroused
spirit which marked the meeting.

"Former Gov. Benton McMillin presided over
the assembly and introduced the speakers. More
than 300 men and women, including some of the most
prominent men and women in Tennessee and the
South, packed the auditorium at the hotel to express
their protest against the slurs cast upon their great
war president and his wife. . . . Speakers at

the meeting unanimously declared that statements made by Mr. Minnigerode in his article tending to show that Rachel Jackson was an uncultured woman and that Andrew Jackson was a 'backwoods bully' were not founded on fact and that such statements were either the work of a misinformed, careless writer, or deliberately perpetrated through prejudice. All who addressed the assembly declared that retraction must be obtained in order that the world might know the truth about President and Mrs. Jackson. The opinion was expressed by all that the work of obtaining a retraction of the statements in Minnigerode's article should proceed in an orderly fashion and that violent indignation should not be allowed to get the upper hand of judgment.

" 'We are here to defend the honor of Andrew Jackson and his wife,' declared Mr. Moore in calling the meeting to order. 'In his lifetime he not only was the greatest man in Tennessee. He was the greatest man of his generation. While he lived, he needed no one to defend his honor or his wife's honor. Now that he is dead, it is our sacred duty and privilege to defend his honor. This is one of the most serious things that ever has come into the history of Tennessee and we want the world to know of our indignation.'

"Mr. Minnigerode's article was scored by Mr. Gaines as 'an invasion of the grave of our beloved and the grave [of] his noble wife.' Mr. Gaines mentioned briefly Jackson's great services to his state and nation. Mr. Gaines heaped vituperation upon the head of Mr. Minnigerode, whom he called a 'mer-

chant of slander, prying open the graves of the dead
in order to sell slander for gold.' The article was
branded by Mr. Gaines as 'vicious, venomous and in-
sidious,' and the speaker called upon the author to
'act like a man and retract his mistakes.' . . .

"Mrs. Stokes declared . . . that it was impossible for any person to visit the Hermitage and believe
that Mrs. Jackson was not a woman of culture. Miss
Gentry declared that a man of Jackson's noble nature never would have selected as his wife a woman
of the type portrayed by Mr. Minnigerode. She
asserted that it was impossible to understand the action of Mr. Minnigerode, who, she asserted, was
[a] minister of the Gospel and a Virginian. . . . 'I
don't care if the man is a preacher, he is a liar,' asserted Dr. Witherspoon, the next speaker. 'His
statements are untrue from start to finish.' . . .

"Mr. Minnigerode was branded by Judge Bell as
a cheap, common, villainous 'prevaricator,' selling his
rough stuff for gold. . . ."

In the same issue, the Nashville *Tennessean* published the resolutions adopted at the meeting, here
reproduced in full.

"Resolved: First, That the Capitol City, inter-
preting the heart and mind, the will and demand of
the citizenship of Tennessee, would remind the outer
world with all the earnestness permitted by the pro-
prieties, that its honored dead are a sacred heritage,
and that its manhood and womanhood resent, and will
forever resent, the effort, come from where it may, to

discredit their worth or to tarnish their memory.

"The portraiture in that article of the victor of New Orleans, the intrepid leader of the Western frontier, whose courage and genius were the bulwarks of civilization: United States District Attorney, judge of the Supreme Court of Tennessee, Congressman and United States Senator, a man twice President of the Republic in its formative period when patriotism and constructive ability were an imperative demand to the national advance and perpetuity; the invincible master-spirit of a great political party, ushered by him into a century of organized active existence, a Tennessean and an American, who by the force of his own personality and principles, his mental and moral courage, inflexible integrity of purpose and of deed, and the splendor of his successes, became a world figure, a man who, as Jefferson said, 'Filled the measure of the country's glory'; the portrayal of such a man as a swash-buckling roysterer, wine-bibbling gamester, and street bully is an indefensible slander which all Tennessee resents, and which the American sense of justice strongly condemns.

"Second: The spirit of the delineation of Rachel Jackson shows that the author preferred to listen to the voice of calumny and the whispers of slander, rather than take audience of the impartial portrayal of history. The attempt to hold up to ridicule and to discredit with innuendo the woman who held sway over the heart of the foremost American of his time and illustrated Christian virtues which ennobled her demeanor in every station, however exalted or ex-

acting, affronts every consideration which should control the public writer or public journal. The inter-
esting thing about Rachel Jackson is not, perchance,
that she could not spell perfectly or meet the requirements of classical English, but that she could capture
the heart and fire the imagination of a man like Jackson and hold his chivalrous devotion until the last
day of her life.

"That Rachel Jackson lacked the power or re-
partee of a woman of the social world, and that her
dancing was not up to the requirements of the min-
uet is trivial and irrelevant; that she could so live
that her distinguished husband could write her epi-
taph in words of noble and restrained tenderness and
grief, through which truth and candor runs like a
golden thread in a rich tapestry, is undying testi-
mony of the intrinsic worth and nobleness of the
woman so deeply, so tenderly loved and cherished.
That one could lay violent hands upon this white
flower of a chivalrous love and devotion is proof
of how alien is the spirit that failed to discern
it."

Signed, "Mrs. Walter Stokes, Regent, Ladies'
Hermitage Association. Mrs. Betty M. Donelson,
President, Andrew Jackson Society. Miss Della
Dortch. John W. Gaines. E. B. Stahlman. George
H. Armistead, Sr. Walter Stokes."

The extent to which these observations and resolutions are justified by the spirit and contents of the
article can best be judged, perhaps, by an examina-

tion of the article itself *in its entirety*—not merely of individual sentences in it divorced from their context—reprinted in the following pages exactly as it was originally written, except for one sentence. In his original version Mr. Minnigerode committed the blunder of stating that Andrew Jackson had shot Mr. Dickinson after the latter's pistol had stopped at half-cock. This statement was entirely incorrect since it was Andrew Jackson's pistol which stopped at half-cock on the first shot. The error was immediately admitted by Mr. Minnigerode as soon as it had been brought to his attention, in a communication sent to Nashville by the editors of the magazine, giving Mr. Minnigerode's authorities; and in the present version the necessary correction has been made.

Up to the present time, December, 1925, no copy of the resolutions passed at Nashville in May, other than that printed in the Nashville *Tennessean,* has ever reached Mr. Minnigerode; no specific criticisms of his article—except those concerning the Dickinson episode—have ever been submitted to him. It is a little difficult, therefore, for Mr. Minnigerode to determine in what respect, other than that no doubt manifested in his original recital of the Dickinson duel, he may have proved himself a "coward, liar, cur and rascal," an interpreter of "contemptuous and narrow prejudices," a "merchant of slander," a "cheap, common, villainous prevaricator selling his rough stuff for gold" and a layer of "violent hands upon this white flower of a chivalrous love and devotion." Or, as certain individuals have not hesitated to suggest, a subsidized political hackwriter. In general, however, one gets the impression that Mr. Minnigerode was less surprised by the outbreak of the fundamentalist attitude towards biographical writing which greeted his article than by the astonishing lack of courtesy—amounting it would seem in some cases to libel—which adorned the transaction. In certain communities there does appear to survive a mediæval point of view towards the fruits of not altogether unlaborious and unconscientious research, but the matter scarcely requires, one would have imagined, a descent to the more unreticent levels of ungraceful abuse.

At all events, always excepting the question of the pistol at half-cock, Mr. Minnigerode has at no time retracted any portion of the article under discussion.—G. P. P.

For the convenience of such readers as may desire it, a partial list of Mr. Minnigerode's authorities is appended.

The *American Encyclopædia.*
The *New International Encyclopædia.*
The *Encyclopædia Britannica.*

F. A. Ogg, *The Reign of Andrew Jackson*, pp. 6, 20, 48, 70.

W. G. Sumner, *Andrew Jackson*, Standard Library of American Statesmen, pp. 5, 12, 13, 16, also Editor's Introduction, p. vii.

Theodore Roosevelt, *Thomas H. Benton*, Standard Library of American Statesmen, p. 24.

J. S. Bassett, *Andrew Jackson*, Vol. I, pp. 8, 12, 21, 22.

James Parton, *Andrew Jackson*, Vol. III, pp. 159-161.

RACHEL JACKSON

1

UNTIL General Jackson secured the presidency, there had been only one widower at the White House—Mr. Jefferson, whose lady never even saw the edifice. Mrs. Jackson, who saw it once, and who was packing her trunks to be taken there, was never to reach it. The first essentially plain, simple, quite commonplace woman of the people to achieve the privilege of residence in the great house at Washington City, Rachel Jackson was not permitted to take her place in that line of distinguished First Ladies— Mrs. Adams, Mrs. Madison, Mrs. Monroe, Mrs. John Quincy Adams—as a successor to whom she would inevitably have furnished so fascinating a contrast; so fascinating for the spectator, so fruitful, no doubt, for the historian, so mortifying, perhaps in many instances, for her entourage, and for herself, almost certainly, so painful. And yet, in her own milieu, in the midst of her own devoted friends, and on three occasions at least in the precarious glare of an unaccustomed public scrutiny, Rachel Jackson was altogether admirable . . .

In 1779, when Captain James Roberston set out from the "settlements" to establish his colony on the Cumberland, in Western Tennessee, he left to his friend, Colonel John Donelson of Virginia, the task of bringing to their appointed destination the families of those adventurous men who had cast their lot with his. Colonel Donelson had been a well to do iron master in Pittsylvania County, a member of the Virginia House of Burgesses, a vestryman, and a personage of some importance. He had come, it was said, to Eastern Tennessee because the marriage of one of his daughters to a hammerer in the Donelson furnaces had brought upon him the social contumely of his home counties. Faced, now, with the necessity of transporting, under inadequate male escort, these colonist families—these amazing pioneer women and their children—from Jonesboro to the Cumberland through an unfamiliar region infested with savages, Colonel Donelson decided to make the entire journey by water. It had never been done before, and it was to take them, down stream and up river, two thousand unknown miles.

He had with him, in his own family, his wife, a married daughter and her husband—possibly the hammerer—and a younger daughter, Rachel, born in 1767 back in Virginia; a girl of twelve, therefore, a black haired, black eyed minx, nimble of foot, gay, sparkling, intrepid and as pretty as you please. With her Virginia upbringing, she must have known all there was to be learned about cookery and the needle; but there had not been much time for books, the family had been on the move, and now there was this adventure to the wilderness, and at the end of it the necessarily unlettered life of a rude frontier. It was unfair, perhaps, that this child should in time have been expected to fill the most exalted social position in the land, and yet it was a very splendid justification of that life of unsurpassed courage and fortitude, a very seemly recognition of that frontier's sturdy nobility. In after years, when they laughed at her, and scorned her, Rachel Donelson must surely have thought of that childhood journey to the Cumberland, and of the days that followed, and smiled proudly. Although, at first, it must have seemed a great lark to her.

But it was not to be a lark, this expedition down the Holston to the Tennessee, down the Tennessee to the Ohio, up the Ohio to the Cumberland, and up the Cumberland to the new settlement which was to be known as Nashville. They started in a winter season of exceptional severity, "in the good boat *Adventure*," to be joined later by other vessels, and it was not until four months later, on April 24, 1780, that the survivors reached Captain Robertson's log cabins. There was the cold, there were the perils of rocks, and shoals, and swollen rivers, there were short rations and a bitter weariness, and there were Indians at every turn. At the junction of the Tennessee and Ohio, the situation was—

"truly disagreeable. The river is very high and the current rapid . . . our provisions exhausted; the crews almost worn down with hunger and fatigue; and know not what distance we have to go or what time it will take us to reach our place of destination."

There was even smallpox, and when the infected ship dropped astern it was no comfort to learn afterwards that the Indians who had captured her themselves caught the disease and died by hundreds.

But the settlement prospered, in spite of famines and savages, and Colonel Donelson prospered with it. He accumulated lands, negroes, cattle and horses, and was accounted wealthy. Rachel grew into spirited young womanhood, and had no equal on a horse in all that western country, or on any dance floor when the fiddles began to scrape. And in 1783 or 4, they all went on a trip to Kentucky, and there, in Mercer County, she married Lewis Robards. Colonel Donelson went back to the Cumberland without her, and in 1785 he was found in the woods, done to death by Indians.

2

And in Kentucky, things were not going so well. Rachel Robards was not the sort of girl to remain inconspicuous, there was nothing demure about her, nothing retiring or submissive. She liked a good time, and she never failed to attract attention. Her husband, Captain Robards, was well educated, a handsome, passionate, tyrannical devil, consumed with jealousy. According to him—although no one, not even his mother, believed him—his wife was not behaving with that discretion which he had a right to expect. There were dreadful scenes, and finally, in 1788, a separation was agreed upon and Rachel's brother, Samuel, came to take her home.

In the midst of this domestic fracas Mrs. Robards senior had been keeping a boarding house, and when, later in the year, one of her young law students decided to try his luck in Western Tennessee, the entire Robards family besought him to use his influence with Rachel in order to bring about a reconciliation. Captain Robards was unhappy, he admitted that his suspicions had been groundless, he promised to be more sensible in future—if only Rachel would come back to him. Mr. Overton reached Nashville early in 1789; he took lodgings in the commodious blockhouse in which the widow

Donelson was also receiving boarders—more for the sake of protection against the Indians, perhaps, than for financial profit—he gave his messages to Rachel, and found her amenable to her husband's entreaties. Word was sent to Captain Robards—and soon afterwards a young man called Andrew Jackson came to live at Mrs. Donelson's in the same cabin room with Mr. Overton, where, for a time, they even shared the same bed.

He had arrived in Nashville a few months before, this Mr. Andrew Jackson, a young lawyer in the train of Judge McNairy. He was twenty-two years old, tall, thin, blue eyed, auburn haired, cadaverous and peppery, and in North Carolina they had just been saying of him that he was "the most roaring, rollicking, game cocking, card playing, mischievous fellow that ever lived in Salisbury." He was absolutely fearless, hopelessly impetuous, an accomplished horseman, a crack shot, irascible as a wasp, touchy as a powder magazine where his honor was concerned—and that of every lady was his—profane, dissipated and altogether fascinating. He lived in one cabin of Mrs. Donelson's blockhouse, and Rachel Robards in the other. They saw each other frequently.

Captain Robards came to his mother-in-law's during the summer of 1789; there was a touching reconciliation, the reunited pair decided to remain at

RACHEL JACKSON

From an engraving by Buttre

the blockhouse—and in a very few months the unfortunate Captain was in tantrums of renewed jealousy. The entire establishment was made aware of the scenes to which he subjected his wife, the whole enclosure rang with the recriminations in which, quite unjustly, he coupled her name with Mr. Jackson's.

"As much commotion and unhappiness prevailed in the family," Mr. Overton recorded, "as in that of Mrs. Robards in Kentucky. At length I communicated to Jackson the unpleasant situation of living in a family where there was so much disturbance, and concluded by telling him that we would endeavor to get some other place."

Whereupon, as might have been expected, Mr. Jackson went blundering into an interview of remonstrance with the angry husband. The two men stood near the orchard fence, and Mr. Jackson was so untactful as to tell Captain Robards that if *he* had had such a wife he would not willingly have brought a tear to her beautiful eyes. Captain Robards promptly offered to horsewhip Mr. Jackson. Mr. Jackson, for his part, offered to meet Captain Robards on the duelling ground. Finally, Captain Robards exclaimed that he did not give a damn for any of them, and that he would not live any longer with Rachel. Mr. Jackson transplanted himself to

Mausker's boarding house, and, in 1790, Captain
Robards went riding back, alone, to Kentucky.

But not long afterwards a rumor reached them
that the Captain was coming back for the purpose
of forcing his wife to accompany him to Kentucky.
Rachel was frightened; Captain Robards had
threatened to "haunt" her, and after "two fair trials"
she was determined not to see him again. It was
decided that she should go to her sister at Natchez,
and an old family friend, Colonel Stark, was chosen
to be her escort. Because of his ability as an Indian
fighter, Mr. Jackson was commanded to make one
of the party—a reluctant Lancelot. He was in love
with Rachel, of course, and confided as much to Mr.
Overton. It must have been a trying journey for
them both. However, soon after Mr. Jackson's return to Nashville, in the summer of 1791, he learned
that Captain Robards had obtained a divorce from
the Virginia Legislature. Mr. Overton, who was
visiting old Mrs. Robards in Kentucky, also heard
the news. Mr. Jackson went straight to Mrs. Donelson and expressed his intention of marrying
Rachel.

"Would you sacrifice your life to save my child's
good name?" she asked him.

"Ten thousand lives, Madam, if I had them!" Mr.
Jackson is supposed to have replied. Nathan Hale
had not been more positive.

They were married that summer, in Natchez.

3

They went to live at Hunter's Hill, thirteen miles
out of Nashville. Mr. Jackson was United States
Attorney for the State, and, when he was not busy
fighting Indians, he found plenty to do, riding circuit through the Tennessee wilderness, and admin-
istering his office with a wealth of straightforward
common sense which made up for the legal refinements which he may have lacked. Aside from that,
he loved horses and gambling, he had his favorite
fighting cocks, he caroused a little on Saturdays at
the Nashville Inn, he swore tremendous oaths to
the evergreen envy of his contemporaries, he swag-
gered up and down the public square and dared anyone to tread on the tail of his coat, he was a leading
citizen. And he trafficked in cattle, axes and cow-
bells, which were the accepted currency of the region, and bought land—two-twenties, six-forties—
too much land, in fact, which he sold to Mr. Allison
of Philadelphia in exchange for notes endorsed to
purchase a stock of goods for a general merchandise
store; so that later, when Mr. Allison went bank-
rupt, Mr. Jackson was in serious difficulties.

But in December, 1793, there was trouble of a far
more dreadful sort. It was Mr. Overton who first
heard the news. That divorce in 1791 had never

been granted. The Virginia Legislature had simply authorized Captain Robards to bring suit in Mercer County, Kentucky. Technically speaking, Mr. Jackson had been living for two years with another man's wife. And now, at last, Captain Robards was suing, on the inevitable grounds. The divorce was duly obtained, this time, and there was nothing for the Jacksons to do but go through a second ceremony of marriage. There is no more striking proof, perhaps, of the impetuosity of Mr. Jackson's character, and of his slender knowledge of the law, than that he should not in the first place have satisfied himself concerning the Virginia statute, and assured himself of the validity of the original report, before offering his ten thousand lives in defence of Rachel Robards's good name. It was an unpardonable lapse on his part; for while at the moment the matter did not attract any more attention than it deserved—there was no question of any moral blame—as the years passed, and Mr. Jackson was more and more in the public eye, the miserable business was revived and made use of as campaign slander, and at the end it served unquestionably as a contributing cause of Rachel Jackson's death. . . .

But in 1794, no one thought anything about it, and in 1796 Mr. Jackson was sent to Philadelphia, to the Congress. He seemed very uncouth, extremely unkempt, and of such a fiery temperament, but he made some good friends—and especially Mr. Edward Livingston, who was still to migrate to New Orleans—and in 1797 he was back again, as Senator this time. But the solemnities of the Senate were too much for him; he resigned his seat, was appointed, in 1798, to the Supreme Court of Tennessee, and, with two partners, undertook the management of the projected store, at Clover Bottom near the racetrack. At the same time, his military activities did not cease, and in 1802 he received his commission as Major General of Militia. As for Rachel, she stayed at home and managed the farm, and when the General was not parading, or when the Judge was not holding court, or when the Storekeeper was not tending his counter, she had him there by her side, and that was all she asked.

4

He left the Bench in 1804, and there was trouble again. The Allison affair had brought financial distress—and the store was on its last legs—and, in order to meet accumulating debts, Hunter's Hill and many of the slaves had to be sold. The Jacksons moved to a small plantation eight miles from Nashville, and there the General built a two story blockhouse of three rooms, to which he soon added a smaller building connected by a passage. He called the place the Hermitage. In this modest home they lived until

1819; the General busy with his fields and his cotton, his cattle and his thoroughbred horses; Rachel occupied with her domestic cares, her kitchen and her dairy.

And in this modest home she dispensed a simple, generous hospitality which was famed throughout the State; a hospitality which found room, somehow, for whole families at a time, and for every peddler who chanced upon the road. She was already a stout little body, but she could still dance reels and country dances with the best of them; she was gay and jolly; she had an astonishing memory and told a good story; and all the children in the neighborhood came to "Aunt Rachel" to hear about the early days on the Cumberland, and about the Indians, and about Daniel Boone who had once passed that way. And after dinner she sat beside the General, in front of the fireplace, and smoked her long reed pipe, and sometimes she handed it to a guest with a cheery, "Honey, won't you take a smoke?"

They were tremendously happy; but there were no children, and they were both so fond of children. And so, in 1809, they adopted one of a pair of twin Donelson nephews, and called him Andrew Jackson junior; and a little later another nephew, Andrew Jackson Donelson, was brought to the Hermitage, where he grew up and was educated at the General's expense, until in time he went to West Point and became a soldier too. It was a busy, kindly, perhaps rather noisy household, certainly not very elegant, but great hearted and charitable.

And sometimes important people came. Colonel Burr came; he came several times, in 1805 and in 1806, and stayed at the Hermitage. The General's merchandise firm was busy preparing boats and supplies for that mysterious expedition of the Colonel's —concerning which it was said that he had written to Mr. Clay that "the executive of the United States are acquainted with my object and view it with complaisance"—and the two men had much to discuss. But later on people began to say queer things about Colonel Burr, and Rachel received him one day very coldly, and the next thing they knew he had been arrested for treason. And because of his boats and supplies, the General was summoned to Richmond as a witness—but they never let him testify, because it turned out that he was convinced that Colonel Burr was not a traitor, and that General Wilkinson was a scoundrel, and that Mr. Jefferson was a despicable cheat. And perhaps the General was right. . . .

And sometimes the General went away and got into trouble. He was always quarrelling, and vituperating, and fighting. With Mr. Sevier, at whom he took pot shots in the public square at Knoxville; with Mr. Dickinson whom he pronounced to be a "worthless, drunken, blackguard scoundrel," and finally killed, quite deliberately although severely wounded himself, on a May morning after his own pistol had stopped once at half cock; with Mr. Dinsmore, whom he called a great many extravagant names; with Mr. Benton, whom he threatened to horsewhip, and whose brother, Jesse, nearly killed him in a disgraceful brawl in the presence of all Nashville. He came home to Rachel half dead from loss of blood that time. In fact, the General was thinking of removing to the Mississippi—he had so many enemies, and so black a reputation!

And what did Rachel think of it all—what did she think of her rowdy, calamitous bravo of a husband? She adored him. She rebuked him for his sins, she strove with him for his unbelieving soul, she lamented his godless tongue and the fatal celerity of his trigger finger, but she adored him. He was "the General," he was "Mr. Jackson," he was her pride and her delight. Perhaps she realized that many of his quarrels were the result of an attempted slur upon what he considered her "sacred name."

"My dear Husband," she wrote to him in 1813 during one of his military expeditions, and the spelling and punctuation are her own, since it is useless to pretend that she was not illiterate, "I received your affectionate Letter. . . . It was the greatest marke of your attention and regard to me I was happy to Here you wer in good health that I Should Shortely

Bee blest with my Dearer Self once more meete you In this Life never an other painfull Separation—But I Saw a Letter you wrote Genl. overton Wherein you Expresst a wish to go to the Northw. Oh how hard it appeard and one to Colo Warde of the same tennure how Can you wish Such a perilous tower but the Love of Country the thirst for Honour and patriotism is your motive—After a feeble acknowledgment of the maney polite and friendly atentions I have received through your goodness by your Friends I shall Never forgit. . . . Shall I see you in twenty Days o God send Showers on Scorching withering grass will not be more reviving Gladly will I meete you when ever you bid me our farm Looks well I Could write you all Day Long but such a Pen I feare you never Can read it pray my Dear write me on the way home—and may The Lord bless you health safely restore you to my armes in mutuel Love is the prayers of your affectionate wife Rawchel Jackson."

5

Rachel did not like it when the General was away, and from now on he was to be away a great deal. Early in 1813, already, he had been called to lead an abortive expedition to the south—that expedition to Mobile which "the heart of Western Tennessee" accompanied down the river and which the machinations of the War Department put an end to at Natchez—and then, in the fall, there came news of the Creek massacre at Fort Mims, and the General was

off again; in good earnest this time, to an arduous
campaign during which, in the midst of manifold military tribulations, he suffered constantly from that
chronic intestinal trouble of his, and at the close of
which Fort Mims was avenged and the power of the
Creeks destroyed.   For Rachel, they were months of
anxiety, of pathetic fears and dismal loneliness.

"My dearest Life," she wrote on one occasion—and
once more one prefers to reproduce the letter in its
original form, so much more genuine and touching
does it seem than if a more perfect syntax and ortho-
graphy had shorn it of its breathless, devoted errors
—"I received your letter by Express. Never shall I
forgit it I have not slept one night since. . . . I
Cryed aloud and praised my god For your safety
how thankfull I was . . . My dear pray let me con-
jur you by every Tie of Love of friendship to let me
see you before you go againe I have borne it untill
now it has thrown me into feavours I am very un-
well—my thoughts is never diverted from that dreadfull scene oh how dreadfull to me and the mercy and
goodness of Heaven to me you are spared perils and
Dangers so maney troubles . . . I cannot sleepe all
can come home but you I never wanted to see you so
mutch in my life . . . let me know and I will fly on the
wings of the purest affection I must see you pray my
Darling never make me so unhappy for aney Country. . . .

"You have now don more than any other man ever
did before you have served your country long enough

You have gained many Laurels You have bind them and more gloriously than had your situation have been differently and instid of your enemyes injuring of you as theay intended it has been an advantage to you you have been gon a long time six months in all that time what has been your trialls daingers and Diffyculties hardeships oh Lorde of heaven how can I beare it . . . our Dear Little Son is well he sayes maney things to swet papa . . . health and happy Days untill we meete—Let it not be Long from your Dearest friend and faithfull wife untill Death."

He had served his country long enough, she thought; actually, he had scarcely begun. He was home in April, 1814, but the war with England went on; in May, he received his commission as Major General in the regular army; in August he was on his way to Mobile. And on December 2, in his old blue cloak, and a leather cap, and tremendous boots flopping around his knees, he came ashore at Bayou St. Jean, where his old friend Mr. Edward Livingston, and Mr. Bernard de Marigny, and several other distinguished gentlemen of New Orleans were waiting to receive him.

There is no space in these pages, naturally, for any discussion of the military operations against the English around New Orleans which culminated in the great, smashing victory of January 8, 1815—a posthumous victory, so to speak, since peace had already been signed with England. Perhaps the General's greatest victory was won—with Colonel Livingston always at his side—in New Orleans itself, in that proud city filled with strange tongues which he found means to inspire with an active devotion to himself; in the midst of those stately Creole grandees—Pontalbas, Villerés, Kernions, Borés, Marignys, d'Estrehans—whose vigorous loyalty to an allegiance only recently established must have gained something of its spirit from his own compelling personality; in the presence of those great Creole ladies, fine flowers of two ancient European aristocracies, gathered in their meticulous drawing rooms to test the nature of the frontiersman from Tennessee whom they found to be a "prince" of chivalry and simple courtesy.

Of course, they quarrelled with him a good deal after the battle. He was rude to the Legislature and impertinent to the civil Governor; he would not alter the rigors of martial law; he would not accept the preliminary news of the peace, and kept the Creole militia under arms; when they began registering at the French Consul's he ordered them all out of town; when a member of the Assembly protested he clapped him in jail; when the Federal Judge issued a writ of habeas corpus he clapped *him* in jail; when the District Attorney applied to the State Judge for another writ he had them both arrested; he behaved in a highly volcanic and tempestuous manner, and eventually found himself summoned for contempt of court before a rabble of military partisans—troopers, "dirty shirts," pirates from Barataria—who dragged him in his carriage to the Exchange Coffee House afterwards in noisy and somewhat undignified triumph. But in spite of it all, people liked him. He had saved the city, he was a hero, he was entitled to his temperamental fireworks. He was just a soldier, a wild American from Tennessee. He must have made them laugh a great deal. They were never to forget him, never to cease thinking of him—most of them—with admiration and affection.

In that circumstance, surely, is to be found his greatest victory, a victory over proud, diffident hearts —but his was as nothing, after all, compared to that other victory, a similar victory won during the last weeks of his dictatorship by a little dumpy woman from Nashville.

Already in December there had been question of Rachel's coming to New Orleans.

"I have not received a letter or paper from Tennessee since the last of October," the General wrote to a friend on December 23. "I am anxious to know whether Mrs. Jackson has sailed from Nashville, under the expectation that she has has been the reason why I have not wrote her. If she is still at home say to her the reason I have not wrote her and say to her and my little son God bless them. I am more than anxious to see them."

Rachel had not yet started in December, but in March she came, finally, bringing with her little Andrew junior.

She came; to a city greater than any which her eyes had ever gazed upon, into the midst of a society distinguished for the grace and elegance of its manners, the splendor and gaiety of its daily intercourse, the costly perfection of its dress, the courtly precision of its speech; she came, and so conspicuously, a little brown skinned woman in dowdy clothes, clumsy tongued, ignorant of the world's decorum, to no manner born save that of the blockhouse and the farm. She came just as she was, with only the reflected glory of her husband's achievement to render more difficult, if anything, the emergencies of her position—into those mansions of the *vieux carré,* of the old Faubourg Marigny, to those Creole homes on Chartres Street, and Bourbon, and Dumaine—and won her astonishing victory. A personal victory which triumphed over custom and prejudice, the victory of her own great heart, of her sweet, charitable nature.

They helped her, of course, those fine Creole ladies; they told her what to do, they brought her clothes to wear; with gentle words and ministering hands they set the seal of their own splendidly generous loyalty, their magnificent conception of the obligations of nobility, upon her goings out and comings in. They would have done this for any *Madame la Générale,*

punctiliously and coldly; for Rachel they did it with
warm kindliness, because they liked her. They stood
in a stately row behind her chair and watched the ap-
proaches to her dignity, guarded the portals of her
negligent tongue. And none more so than Mrs.
Edward Livingston; beautiful Louise d'Avezac, a
Creole belle from Santo Domingo, a widow at sixteen,
a refugee from the black massacre in the Colony, and
now the wife of Louisiana's great jurist who was
one day to be Mr. Jackson's Secretary of State—
how little they dreamed it then—the mistress of his
house on Chartres Street, and one of the most cherished adornments of the fastidious Faubourg. With
Louise Livingston at her side, Rachel could do no
wrong.

She did make them all laugh very heartily, though,
and especially at that great ball at the Exchange,
when—

"after supper we were treated to a most delicious
pas de deux by the conqueror and his spouse. To
see these two figures, the General, a long, haggard
man with limbs like a skeleton, and *Madame la Générale,* a short, round dumpling, bobbing opposite each
other like half drunken Indians to the wild melody of
'Possum up de Gum Tree', and endeavoring to make
a spring into the air, was very remarkable and far
more edifying a spectacle than any European ballet
could possibly have furnished."

There is no more pleasant a scene in all the annals of the day. One imagines her in her lace cap, smiling and perspiring, skirts in hand, wearing the topaz jewelry presented to her by the ladies of the town.

So Rachel came to New Orleans, and after a while departed, honored and much beloved. . . .

6

The homeward journey of the Jacksons, in April, 1815, was a continued triumph of banquets, swords of honor and public acclamations, in the midst of which Rachel was probably very glad to see again the familiar outlines of her Hermitage. But there was to be very little rest for the General. There was a trip to Washington, to explain his New Orleans arrests; he was appointed to the command of the Army of the South; and then, late in 1817, he was ordered to Fort Scott, to chastise the Seminoles in Florida who had been persecuting American settlers. And the Reverend Gideon Blackburn began to preach in Nashville.

Whether or not his instructions sanctioned an invasion of West Florida—and there was a tremendous argument about it afterwards—the General was temperamentally unable to find himself in that locality without capturing Pensacola; he had already captured it once on his own initiative, and now, in May, 1818, he captured it again and presented the whole

ANDREW JACKSON

From a contemporary print

Florida territory at the point of his sword to a somewhat embarrassed administration which had been negotiating with Spain for its purchase. The public clamor of approval over the event was not the least annoying feature of the Government's dismay at the pranks of its military *enfant terrible*. There was a frightful to-do about it in Washington, and Mr. Monroe, and Mr. Calhoun, and Mr. John Quincy Adams talked themselves green in the face while the General was being fêted in New York and Philadelphia, but in the end it all blew over, and the Hero returned to Nashville to superintend the construction of a new Hermitage.

It was a fine two story brick house, with a double piazza resting on grooved wooden columns, erected on a site chosen by Rachel herself in a field near the original blockhouse. Behind the house was the garden which Rachel was to enjoy so much, and for which he was always procuring rare plants and flowers. The garden in which she was to be buried; not far from the little church which the General soon built for her, for Rachel—partly, perhaps, because of her continued loneliness—had suddenly "gotten religion," strenuous, austere, militant, Presbyterian religion. It had happened along in 1816, under that wave of pioneer preaching which had flooded the frontiers after the war. She may have danced and made merry before, but now the Reverend Gideon

Blackburn, her dear Parson Blackburn, had weaned
her from the profligacy of mundane affairs. "Say to
my father in the Gospel. . . . I shall always love
him as such. Often I have blessed the Lord that I
was permitted to be called under his ministry." As
for the General, he still thought very little of such
matters, but he made no objections to Rachel's somewhat florid devotions, he received her numerous cler-
ical visitors with unfailing good nature, and allowed
himself to be prevailed upon to say grace at meals—
which was a great step forward for Mr. Jackson.

There was a quite different Rachel at the Hermitage now, and salvation hung, so to speak, like the
sword of Damocles above the General's unreceptive
head—but first there was a task to be accomplished
at Pensacola. The treaty with Spain had at last
been ratified; Colonel Forbes had been sent to Havana to secure the Florida archives—only he failed
to secure them; with the record of General Jackson's
turbulent governorship of New Orleans fresh in his
mind, and the knowledge that no more precarious
choice could possibly be made for a position demanding the utmost patience and tact, Mr. Monroe
appointed the General to be Governor of Florida and
to preside at the formalities of transfer. Perhaps
Mr. Monroe did this in order to get even with Mr.
Jackson—he had conquered the Floridas, now let him
govern them.

At all events, on April 18, 1821, the Governor and his Lady, with the two boys, left Nashville for the South. He was empowered with all the authority formerly residing in the Captain General of Cuba and the Spanish governors of East and West Florida. It seemed to be a generous mandate, and a great many personal friends, to say nothing of a host of perfect strangers, packed their valises and followed in the wake of so brilliantly promissory a patronage. . . .

7

The Jacksons went down the river to New Orleans, where they were received with tremendous festivities —but it was a very different New Orleans now in Rachel's enlightened eyes, this city in which she had once danced so blithely.

"It reminds me," she wrote, "of those words in Revelations: 'Great Babylon is come up before me.' Oh the wickedness, the idolatry of this place! Unspeakable the riches and splendor. . . The attention and honors paid to the General far excel a recital by my pen. They conducted him to the Grand Theatre. . . . Songs of praise were sung by ladies and in the midst they crowned him with a crown of laurel. The Lord has promised his humble followers a crown that fadeth not away; the present one is already withered, the leaves are falling off. . . . I know I never was so tried before, tempted, proved in all things. . . . Oh for Zion! I wept when I saw this idolatry. . . .

I have written you this through the greatest bustle and confusion. The nobility have assembled to escort the General with a full band of martial music to review the troops. . . . Oh farewell! Pray for your sister in a heathen land, far from my people and church. . . . "

Yes. They pushed on; to Mobile, where they stayed nine days; to Mount Pelier, where they waited five weeks for Colonel Forbes who did not come with the archives; and finally, on June 17, to the house of a Spanish gentleman, fifteen miles from Pensacola, "that city of contention" which so resented their coming. Rachel did not like Florida; she thought it greatly overrated, nothing but sweet potatoes and yams, and a thousand acres of its soil could not match one "of our fine Tennessee land." And she was worried about her chickens at home. In other respects,

"Oh how shall I make you sensible of what a heathen land I am in. . . . Often I think of the Babylonian captivity. . . . Oh, I feel as if I was in a vast howling wilderness, far from my friends in the Lord, my home and Country. The Sabbath entirely neglected and profaned. . . ." And again, "Oh for Zion! I am not at rest, nor can I be, in a heathen land. . . . How happy and thankful should you be in a land of gospel light and liberty. . . . Do not be uneasy for me. 'Although the vine yield no fruit and the olive no oil, yet will I serve the Lord.' Adieu, adieu."

Religion, the harsh religion of her day, had come to Rachel, and darkened for her the whole green, sunlit world. One begins to appreciate the amazing influence of the good Parson Blackburn and his itinerant companion prophets of woe, to realize the grim bigotry of that old camp meeting fanaticism, to see foreshadowed the growth in the land of that intolerant piety which was to sway the minds of generations of persons far less unintelligent, many of them, than Rachel Jackson.

She moved into town with the two boys, to a pleasant house on Main Street, adorned with galleries from which there was a view of the bay and enlivened by "the finest sea breeze . . . so exhilerating, so pure, so wholesome." But many of the houses looked in ruins, "old as time," and the city squares were overgrown with shrubs, weeping willows and the Pride of China, so neglected, like the flowers growing wild in the abandoned gardens. And it rained and rained, until sometimes the streets were two feet deep in water. And the inhabitants, who spoke nothing but French and Spanish,

"such a mixed multitude. . . there are fewer white people far than any other, mixed with all nations under the canopy of heaven, almost in nature's darkness. But thanks to the Lord that has put grace in this his servant to issue his proclamation. . . . I think the sanctuary is about to be purged for a minister of the gospel to come over to the help of the Lord in this dark region."

At all events, she changed the Spanish Sabbath for them. She had not been "an idle spectator" during her first Sundays in Pensacola—"the Sabbath profanely kept, a great deal of noise and swearing in the streets, shops kept open, trade going on, I think, more than on any other day." Naturally. But she arranged it differently for the future, by her own commands, and "had the happiness of witnessing the truth of what I had said. Great order was observed; the doors kept shut; the gambling houses demolished; fiddling and dancing not heard any more on the Lord's day, cursing not to be heard. . . ." Fiddling and dancing not heard any more. They hated her. Just as they hated her fiery, incomprehensible General, *Don* Andrew Jackson, *Gubernador*.

8

He rode into town, looking very pale and solemn, at the head of the American troops, at seven o'clock on the morning of July 17. Down Main Street, under Rachel's balcony, to the Government House where the Spanish governor, *Don* Callava, was waiting for the formal substitution of flags. There was a dinner afterwards, for all the officials, and the Spanish garrison was embarked for Havana. The streets were lined with American land speculators and office

seekers, and thronged with natives who wept to see
the passing of their old allegiance, this exchange of
old Spain for new America. Except for the American opportunists, it was not a cheerful scene.

"The whole town was in motion," Rachel observed.
"Never did I ever see so many pale faces. . . . There
were no shouts of joy or exultation; but on the contrary we sympathized with these people. . . oh how
they burst into tears to see the last ray of hope departed of their devoted city and country. . . . How
did the city sit solitary and mourn. Never did my
heart feel more for any people. Being present, I entered immediately into their feelings. Their manners,
laws and customs, all changed, and really a change
was necessary."

Rachel was convinced of that. The Lord, she
thought,

"had a controversy with them. They were living far
from God. If they would have the gospel of Jesus
and his apostles, it would have been otherwise, but
they would not. The field is white for harvest, but
where are the laborers? Not one. Oh for one of
our faithful ministers to come and impart the word
of life to them."

In St. Augustine, a Methodist missionary had begun
distributing tracts under the very eye of the Cath-
olic Priest as soon as the American flag had been
run up, but not so at Pensacola; even in September,

"not one minister of the gospel has come to this place yet, no, not one."

But whatever the nature of the Lord's controversy with the Pensacolans, *Don* Andrew soon had one of his own. *Don* Callava could not make up his mind to fulfill the terms of the treaty and remove himself; he prevaricated, he procrastinated, he conspired to annoy the General in as many ways as possible with Mr. Eligius Fromentin, a Federal Judge—and *Don* Andrew did not like Federal Judges—and with Mr. John Innerarity, a Mobile trading agent much beholden to the Spaniards for past favors.

"I shall not pretend to describe the toils, fatigue and trouble," Rachel sighed in August. "Those Spaniards had as leave die as give up their country. He has had terrible scenes; the governor has been put in the calaboose, which is a terrible thing, really. I was afraid there would be a rebellion."

It was quite true. *Don* Callava had been put in the calaboose, with two of his minions, and Judge Fromentin had tried to issue a writ of habeas corpus, which was a fatal thing to do as long as the General retained his health. It was all because of a lawsuit brought by the heirs of a certain Nicholas Maria Vidal against Mr. Innerarity's house; *Don* Callava had refused to surrender the necessary papers and had been dragged from his bed into the fiery Presence for a

midnight interview during which all the parties concerned did nothing but shout insulting remarks at
each other; whereupon the scandalized Spaniard had
been hurled into jail, where his friends sought him out
with refreshment and provender, and spent the rest
of the night in song and high merriment, imitating
the *Americano's* tantrums. It was a stupid, childish
fracas, the echoes of which finally dwindled away in
the corridors of the Spanish embassy at Washington
—and in which much was said on both sides—but it
did not serve to popularize *Don* Andrew's somewhat
whimsical regime.

And there was another pebble in the Governor's
shoe. "There never was a man more disappointed
than the General has been," Rachel explained quite
frankly, although the italics are not hers. "In the
first place, he has not the power to appoint one of
his friends, *which, I thought, was in part the reason
of his coming.* He calls it a wild goose chase, his
coming here. . . . Many have been disappointed.
I have not"—although in the intervals of prayer
meetings she had used her influence on behalf of
various office hunters—"I saw it as plain as I now
do when it is passing. . . Many wander about like
lost sheep; all have been disappointed in offices. . . .
The President made all the appointments and sent
them from the city of Washington." The game was
really not worth the candle. "The General, I think,

is the most anxious man to get home I ever saw. . . .
They all begin to think with me that Tennessee is
the best country yet."

And so, in October, 1821, they went home. They
reached Nashville on November 4, and on December
1 the General's resignation went into effect.

9

They were very glad to be home. The General had
not been at all well, and Rachel herself had felt the
effects of the unaccustomed Florida climate; it was
much pleasanter to stay quietly at the Hermitage,
listening to the young people's fun—all the nieces
and nephews who filled the place—or playing the
piano in the evening for the General while he rendered *Money Musk,* and *Fisher's Hornpipe,* and
Auld Lang Syne on the flute; or to drive through
the lovely Tennessee countryside in the big carriage
behind the four grey horses, with the footmen in blue
liveries and glazed hats with silver bands. Rachel
would have been content to go on doing this all her
life—and trying to convert the General. But before
very long there was something quite different—and
to Rachel probably quite dismaying—on the carpet.

It had been talked about all year, and in July, 1822,
the Tennessee Legislature came right out and nominated the General for the presidency, putting him
forward against the Adams, Crawford, Clay candi-

dacies as a man "calm in deliberation, cautious in decision, efficient in action"—a summary of his qualities
which should have made even Rachel smile. Of all
the most remote possible choices for the office, the
General was perhaps the least well fitted for it, but he
was a popular hero, and the Great Voice began to
make itself heard. In the meantime, the General was
elected to the United States Senate, and when he
returned to Washington for his second session, in the
fall of 1824, he took Rachel with him, travelling in his
coach and four.

And Washington was not at all sure what to do
about Mrs. Jackson. There were queer stories about
her—something concerning her marriage—and she
was said to be such a dowdy. "A dilemma was presented, and a grand debate ensued," Mrs. Seaton reports, "as to whether the ladies would visit her." But
the question of propriety was finally settled, and "all
doubts were laid aside." And as was always the case
whenever Rachel braved the world's inspection, in
spite of her social deficiencies she won all hearts by
her simplicity and sincerity. Her visit, it was recorded, gave—

"a damper to those who have used her as an argument against him. She has proven the falsity of the
thousand slanders which have been industriously cir-
culated of her awkwardness, ignorance and indecor-
um. I . . . find her striking characteristics to be

an unaffected simplicity of manners with great goodness of heart. So far from being denied the attentions usually extended to strangers, as was predicted, she has been overpowered by the civilities of all parties."

She thought so herself.

"To tell you of this city," she wrote, "I would not do justice to the subject. The extravagance is in dressing and running to parties, but I must say they regard the Sabbath and attend preaching . . . oh my dear friend, how shall I get through this bustle. There are not less than from fifty to one hundred persons calling in a day. . . . Don't be afraid of my giving way to those vain things. . . . The play actors sent me a letter requesting my countenance to them. No. A ticket to balls and parties. No, not one." But she did go, finally, to General Brown's ball. "Two dinings, several times to drink tea. Indeed, Mr. Jackson encourages me in my course."

They were breathlessly busy, stopping at the same hotel with General Lafayette, and the place was packed all day. And Washington was in a turmoil of pre-election log rolling—Mrs. Crawford and her visits —Mr. Clay and his friends—Mr. Jackson and his banquets—Mr. Clay—Mr. Clay—but the General comported himself with great dignity and avoided intrigue as much as possible. Everyone was in high good humor, and the General had little doubt of the outcome; he had brought Rachel to be there with him on the great day. But he was four years too early.

For on the great day the election was thrown into the House, and Mr. Clay pushed Mr. Adams into the White House. Secretly, Rachel was probably delighted. The Jacksons went home, in March, 1825, to prepare for General Lafayette's visit to the Hermitage. Rachel was going to ask "a number of ladies and farmers from the neighborhood." The General —the General was going to smash Mr. Clay if it took every last breath in his body. Mr. Clay and Mr. Adams. His second presidential campaign began immediately. . . .

10

It was to be one of the most vicious, merciless, scurrilous campaigns in the annals of American politics. From the very first, Mr. Jackson believed that his recent defeat had been contrived as the result of a bargain between Mr. Adams and Mr. Clay, and when the latter was immediately appointed Secretary of State, it was difficult to persuade a large portion of the population that this was not the case. Andrew Jackson had been the popular choice for President, and owing to the intrigues of Mr. Adams and Mr. Clay he had not been elected; so the people reasoned. "Expired at Washington," one newspaper announced, "on the 9th of February, of poison administered by the assassin hands of John Quincy Adams,

the usurper, and Henry Clay—the virtue, liberty
and independence of the United States." Mr. John
Randolph uncoiled himself in the Senate and talked
about the combination of "the Puritan and the Black-
leg." There was a duel, but the phrase could not be
stilled, and the destruction of "bargain and corruption" became the Jacksonian platform.

Mr. Jackson was formally nominated by the Tennessee Legislature in October, 1825, upon the occasion of his resignation from the United States Senate, and throughout the Union the "Friends of General Jackson"—which meant all the enemies of Mr.
Adams and Mr. Clay—began to roll up their sleeves,
and sharpen their quills. Perhaps never before had
there been such a flood of campaign literature, such
a delving into personal records and affairs, such a
slinging of slimy falsehood and filthy abuse. Everything which could be raked up against Mr. Adams
during his phenomenally long career in public office
was sent as grist to the mills of invective; he was even
said, while Minister to Russia, to have given up an
American servant girl of Mrs. Adams's to the Czar.
And anyway, he had—so it was claimed—purchased
a billiard table for the White House, and was it proper that public funds "be applied to the purchase of
gaming tables and gambling furniture?" Certainly
not; such conduct in the Chief Magistrate was
"enough to shock and alarm the religious, the moral

and the reflecting part of the community." Mr. Jackson himself flatly accused Mr. Clay of having sent a Congressman to him with corrupt proposals, and the fact that the Congressman in question just as flatly denied the event made no impression in this "movement of the people," this "revolt of democracy against aristocracy."

And everything which the General had ever done was remembered, and luridly adorned with fanciful embellishments, and screamed at him from one end of the country to the other. All the "vices" which made his private character "so eminently disgusting and sickening to virtuous sensibility." His quarrels, his duels, his gamecocks, his cusswords, his "murder" of deserting militiamen at Mobile, his contempt of court at New Orleans, his insubordinate invasion of Florida, his calaboosings at Pensacola. And his marriage. That was the big talking point, the subject of many venomous pamphlets, the material for countless editorials, the verse and chorus of endless shameful ballads—his marriage. And that brazen hussy, that no account, vulgar, disreputable little frump, his wife. . . .

They managed to keep it from her; she was at the Hermitage still trying to convert the General, and rejoicing in his final promise that he would join the Church as soon as he could do it without its seeming merely a move in this battle of politics which she so disliked; she was not at all well, and there was trouble with her heart; she did not know, did not dream, what they were saying about her. And the General stayed always near her—for he would not consent to any personal electioneering—gaunt, harassed, enraged, infinitely watchful. And in the midst of it all, in this campaign which had passed the limits of any decency, under a provocation too great to be endured, this habitually imprudent, passionate, vindictive man wrote these very estimable words——

"The female character," he told his lieutenants, "should never be introduced by my friends unless a continuation of attack should continue to be made against Mrs. Jackson, and that by way of just retaliation upon the known guilty. My great wish is that it may be altogether evaded if possible by my friends. I never war against females, and it is only the base and cowardly that do."

11

They made one more public journey together, before the election; to New Orleans, for the anniversary of the battle in January, 1828. The General preferred to stay at home during the campaign, but the political significance of the outing was sufficiently obscured by the historic nature of the occasion, in spite of the swarm of politicians from all over the country who joined the party, and so they went. Down the river in the *Pocahontas* to the parades and ban-

RACHEL JACKSON

From a contemporary print

quets at Natchez, where they were met by the reception committee from New Orleans, come to escort them to that abode of heathen idolatry—as it still, no doubt, appeared to Rachel. And on the morning of January 8, to the sound of cannon and bells, in the presence of tumultuous multitudes which blackened the waterfront and hung in clusters in the riggings of ships, they stepped ashore at the levee.

And there, waiting to receive them, were Mr. and Mrs. Bernard de Marigny, in whose sumptuous city residence, in the old Creole Faubourg which they practically owned, the Jacksons were to spend the four days of ceaseless festival which followed. Mr. de Marigny was still incredibly wealthy, famous for his lavish hospitality, distressingly handsome, one of the grandest of the grandees. Mrs. de Marigny was his second wife, the celebrated Anna Mathilde Morales, for whom, having seen her once only at a ball, he had undertaken to fight seven duels in as many days. They were able, Mr. de Marigny remarked later, to give the Jacksons "some pretty entertainments."

One can well imagine, and it is not in any malicious spirit, but rather as a tribute to Rachel's courage, that one ventures to quote a contrasting contemporary Nashville impression of her at this period.

"A coarse looking, stout, little old woman, whom you might easily mistake for [the General's] washerwoman, were it not for the marked attention he pays her. . . . Her eyes are bright and express great kindness of heart; her face is rather broad, her features plain. . . . But, withal, her face is so good-natured and motherly, that you immediately feel at ease with her. . . . Her figure is rather full, but loosely and carelessly dressed, so that when she is seated she seems to settle into herself in a manner that is neither graceful nor elegant."

This was the guest of honor sitting in the brilliant parlor of the Marigny mansion, "with her dowdified figure, her inelegant conversation, and her total want of refinement," while "the ladies of the Jackson party hovered near her at all times, apparently to save her from saying or doing anything which might do discredit to their idol." This was the fantastically inadequate little woman who must soon prepare to take her exalted station in the capital of the Republic.

But after all, "she was really beloved. She was a truly good woman, the very soul of benevolence and kindness." Always, to the end of her days by those who knew her, Rachel Jackson was beloved and respected. The White House would not have required more of her. . . .

12

They went home, the summer passed. Rachel was not very well. The congratulatory messages began

pouring in. Mrs. Cadwalader of Philadelphia wished
to say that "no endeavor will be spared to supply to
Mrs. Jackson the places of those warm friends whom
she will leave behind her."   Mrs. Hayne of Washington would be pleased to make all the necessary ar-
rangements for Mrs. Jackson's comfort before her
arrival. In November, some twelve hundred thousand voters gave the General a majority of one hundred and thirty-nine thousand votes. A magnificent
clamor of popular joy arose upon the midnight air;
a triumphant uproar gave voice to the conviction that
Democracy was restored to the nation in all its native
purity; plans were made for a stupendous celebration
in Nashville on December 23; the Hermitage became
a mad house. Rachel said, "Well, for Mr. Jackson's
sake I am glad, for my own part I never wished it.
. . . I assure you I would rather be a doorkeeper
in the house of my God than to dwell in that palace
in Washington."

She took no pleasure in worldly glories; she did not
want to go to Washington; perhaps, poor soul, she
appreciated the trials which must inevitably await her
there. But it had to be done, and she must go to
Nashville shopping, and to see the trousseau which
the ladies of the town were preparing for her. And
then the dreadful thing happened.

She had finished her city errands, and was sitting
in the back parlor of the inn waiting for her carriage,

when some people entered the front room. They did not know that she was there, and they talked, gaily, sarcastically, cruelly. About her, about her lack of social refinements and the figure that she would cut in Washington, and about the old Robards scandal which had swept the country. Alone, in the little back room, Rachel Jackson learned for the first time that she had become a campaign caricature, that her name had been made a public infamy, that her presence at her beloved General's side had been a handicap to his success. She stayed there quite quietly until they had gone, because she "supposed they did not know I heard them and would be hurt if they found out I had." When she reached the Hermitage, the negroes all said that Missus looked "shot through the heart."

Her poor old heart, which was failing a little after sixty-one years. But her courage never failed. For a long time she would not tell the General what was the matter; although she confided in her niece and begged her to take her place. "I will be no advantage to my husband at the White House," she insisted, "and I wish never to go there and disgrace him. You will go and take care of his house for him, and I will stay here and take care of everything until he comes back." Nothing, one suspects, could have dragged her to Washington now. But her spirit was to be there, for when the General found out, there came into his soul such a hatred of persecution, such a fury of resentment against scandal mongers, such an exalted conception of all womanhood enshrined in his memory, as were to influence the whole course of his first administration, blind him to the shortcomings of a notorious lady of his Cabinet, and alter the destinies of many personages.

On Wednesday morning, December 17, in the midst of her household duties, Rachel had a severe heart attack. They put her to bed, where she remained in considerable pain until the evening of the 19th. She felt better then, and the Saturday and Sunday passed quietly. They persuaded the General, who had scarcely left her side, to take a little rest. On Monday evening, December 22, Rachel was so much improved that at nine o'clock the General retired to an adjoining room, in anticipation of the strenuous festivities prepared for the morrow. Hannah, the maid, came in to make up the bed, and helped Rachel to a chair. There was a sudden cry, and in a few seconds Rachel had expired in Hannahs' arms. The General simply refused to believe that she was dead. He stayed there for hours, trying to revive her.

Hannah herself reported these facts—and yet there is another curious version which states that Rachel had not been ill, and that she died quite suddenly, alone, in the middle of the night. . . .

13

The news was all over Nashville on the morning of December 23. The big dinner was to have taken place that evening, but now "congratulations are turned into expressions of condolence, tears are substituted for smiles, and sincere and general mourning pervades the community." The funeral was on Christmas Eve, in a drizzle of rain, so they had covered the path from the house to the grave with cotton. Some of the ladies had dressed Rachel in white satin, with kid gloves and slippers—part of the trousseau intended for her White House wardrobe. In Nashville, all business was suspended, and the church bells were tolling, while the entire town drove out to the Hermitage. "Such a scene I never wish to witness again. . . . The road to the Hermitage was almost impassable, and an immense number of persons attended the funeral."

They buried her in her garden, where now stands the little white marble dome on pillars, and on a tablet have been inscribed these words——

"Here lie the remains of Mrs. Rachel Jackson, wife of President Jackson, who died the 22nd of December, 1828, aged 61. Her face was fair, her person pleasing, her temper amiable, her heart kind; she delighted in relieving the wants of her fellow creatures, and cultivated that divine pleasure by the most liberal and unpretending methods; to the poor she was a benefactor; to the rich an example; to the wretched a comforter; to the prosperous an ornament; her piety went hand in hand with her benevolence, and she thanked her Creator for being permitted to do good. A being so gentle and so virtuous, slander might wound but could not dishonor. Even death, when he tore her from the arms of her husband, could but transport her to the bosom of God."

Peggy Eaton

PEGGY EATON

1

MRS. EDWARD LIVINGSTON, of Santo Domingo, New Orleans and Washington, was a good friend of General Andrew Jackson; she had stood beside the dowdy Mrs. Jackson in New Orleans, in 1815, and guided her through the perils of that social adventure; when, because of Mrs. Jackson's sudden death in 1828—on the eve, almost, of her husbands inauguration—it became known that the General's niece, Mrs. Donelson, would do the honors of the White House, Mrs. Livingston had immediately offered to assist her in the purchase of a New York and Philadelphia wardrobe more suited to "the air of Washington" than that obtainable at Nashville. But when the Jackson cortege arrived in Washington, in February, 1829—the General, Mr. and Mrs. Andrew Jackson junior, Mr. and Mrs. Andrew Jackson Donelson, and another niece, Miss Eastin, soon to be followed by that Mr. Earl whose sole and continuous duty it was to paint portraits of the President—Mrs. Livingston was not so sure.

There was nothing the matter with the cortege itself; the General had, ordinarily, "the peculiar, rough, independent, free and easy ways of the backwoodsman, but at the same time," Mr. Sargent observed, "he had, whenever occasion required, and especially in the society of ladies, very urbane and graceful manners." Mrs. Jackson junior was very pretty and attractive; Mrs. Donelson was, in the opinion of Mrs. Livingston's daughter, Cora, "a beautiful, accomplished and charming woman, with wonderful tact and delightfully magnetic manners." Though the mother of two children "she might pass for sweet sixteen," and everyone was in love with her.

It was not the cortege that worried Mrs. Livingston. It was the popular flood which came pouring into Washington in its wake; the thousands and thousands of depressingly "plain" people who came from all over the country to jam the taverns and taprooms, and swarm around the Hero in his "Wigwam" at Gadsby's; persons of the slightest education and breeding who made the capital their own, and gave evidence, in countless ungraceful ways, of the fact that the recent presidential election had been a victory of the Common—the very common—People. America's first—for Mr. Jefferson's had been so only vocally—America's first *sans culotte* revolution.

Of course, Mrs. Livingston was a Creole belle, a Frenchwoman born, a creature of exceeding elegance, and, naturally, no dowdy. "Dowdies—dowdies won't do for European courts," Mr. John Randolph told her when her husband was named Minister to France, and she was no dowdy. On the contrary, "the salons of Paris," Mr. Randolph was certain, "must have far greater attractions for her than the yahoos of Washington." That was it, Washington was simply full of yahoos. The pleasant, comfortable seemliness of the long Virginia regime was at an end; Tennessee— one speaks strictly from the point of view of Washington in 1829—Tennessee and the whole frontier West were rolling in, uproariously and crudely. The mob was at Versailles.

Mrs. Samuel Harrison Smith felt the same way about it.

"Never before," she wrote sadly, "did the city seem to me so gloomy—so many changes in society—so many families broken up, and those of the first distinction and who gave a tone to society. Those elegantly furnished houses stripped of their splendid furniture —that furniture exposed to public sale—those drawing rooms, brilliantly illuminated, in which I have so often mixed with gay crowds, distinguished by rank, fashion, beauty, talent—resounding with festive sounds—now empty, silent, dark, dismantled. Oh, 'tis melancholy! Mrs. Clay's, Mrs. Southard's, Mrs. Porter's houses exhibit this spectacle. They are completely stripped—the furniture all sold—the families, for the few days they remained after the sale, un-

comfortably crowded in one little room. The doors
shut on company and only one or two intimate friends
admitted."

The glory was departed. . . .

2

As might have been expected, Mr. Jackson's inauguration was a riot; nothing more disgraceful had
ever been seen in Washington. There was no parade
—nothing to suggest Mr. Clay's disdainful "military
chieftain"—and no semblance of dignity. The General walked to the Capitol, accompanied by a tumultuous crowd which pursued him on foot, in gigs and in
wood carts, and did its best to break down the barriers
in front of the platform; after the ceremony, the
President escaped on horseback to the White House,
leading the way for a rabble which tore after him
down the avenue, animated by the desire to get at
the inaugural refreshments. There followed "a regular Saturnalia" at the Palace. "The mob broke in in
thousands. Spirits black, yellow and grey poured in
in one uninterrupted stream of mud and filth, among
the throngs many subjects for the penitentiary."
It was said afterwards that ten thousand people
had crammed their way into the building. "A rabble, a mob, of boys, negroes, women, children, scram-
bling, fighting, romping." They came in through
the windows, they inundated the whole ground floor,

they stood in their muddy boots on the damask chairs installed by Mr. Monroe during his tenancy; they hurled themselves at the trays of food. "Cut glass and china to the amount of several thousand dollars had been broken in the struggle to get the refreshments . . . ladies fainted, men were seen with bloody noses, and such a scene of confusion took place as is impossible to describe." It was impossible to breathe in the reception room. Mr. Jackson was finally spirited away through a back door; punch was carried out onto the lawn in tubs and buckets, and the people went pouring out through the windows again after it in "a living torrent. It was the People's day, the People's President, and the People would rule."

The mob was at the Tuileries. . . .

It was perhaps the most significant day in American political history, it was the first display of the fundamental absurdity of "democracy" at any price, it was, as it was inevitably bound to be, the rule of the yahoos. To those who could remember, it was not dissimilar in spirit to the French Revolution. There was only lacking the guillotine.

The lack was supplied at once. "What most adds to the general gloom," Mrs. Smith recorded, "is the rumor of a general proscription. Every individual connected with the government . . . is filled with apprehension." Mr. Webster had foreseen it before the General's arrival.

"My opinion is that when he comes he will bring a breeze with him. Which way it will blow I cannot tell. He will either go with the party, as they say in New York, or go the whole hog, as it is phrased elsewhere, making all the places he can for friends and supporters and shaking a rod of terror at his opposers."

That was it—the People had demanded a change in administration, there must consequently, in the immortal words of Mr. Jefferson, be a change in administration. Gadsby's was thronged with office seekers who pushed their way into Mr. Jackson's private chamber and clamored for immediate employment; the public lobbies, the very roadway leading to the White House—after the General moved in —were obstructed by crowds of aspirants to official patronage, determined to "push like the devil." Not one of the old incumbents must remain, not one of Mr. Jackson's supporters must go unrewarded. The Treasury, the Customs, the Postoffice—let them be swept clear of faithful clerks who had spent their whole lives, many of them, in the service, and let their places be given forthwith to democratic voters, for to the victors belonged the spoils.

The word was comparatively new in American politics, and the system which it represented a novelty the delights of which have never since ceased to charm the popular imagination. There had been removals from office before, at the inauguration of a victorious administration, but never to such an extent as darkened the opening days of Mr. Jackson's presidency. "The gloom of suspicion pervaded the face of society. No man deemed it safe and prudent to trust his neighbor, and the interior of the department presented a fearful scene of guarded silence, secret intrigue, espionage and tale bearing." None could tell when the axe would fall, "no one knows who is next to encounter the stroke of death," Mr. Clay wrote. "You have no conception of the moral tyranny which prevails here over those in employment." Families whose existence depended on the salary of men who had made the government service their career found themselves destitute, and in many cases homeless and without any alternative resource; the suspense and distress paralyzed business, and drove some unfortunates to insanity and suicide.

It was the uncertainty that was so terrible, the partisan injustice which took no stock of merit, of work carefully performed in the past, of any claim to benevolent consideration. The actual removals—in the light of later manifestations of the process—were not so numerous; some three hundred offices out of the six hundred at the President's disposal, only six hundred of the available eight thousand postmasters and deputies. But it was the unexpected vindictiveness of it, the treachery and corruption which under-

mined all public life, the shameless rapacity of this
President who already once, when Governor of
Florida, had felt himself aggrieved because of his
inability to appoint his friends to office.

It would have been well enough if the system had
been applied to evil doers, for the purpose of "ferret-
ing out treasury rats" and correcting abuses,

"but it spreads abroad like a contagion: spies, in-
formers, denunciations—the fecula of despotism.
Where there are listeners there will be tale bearers
. . . I had hoped that this would be a national administration"—the writer was a man friendly to the
Jackson regime—"but it is not even an administration
of a party. Our republic, henceforth, will be gov-
erned by factions, and the struggle will be who shall
get the offices and their emoluments."

The guillotine was set up, the American Reign of
Terror was under way. . . .

3

And in the meantime, already before the inauguration—when he was not busy rejecting opportunities
of marriage presented by numerous enterprising
ladies, "most of them over forty, and a number in
the advance of sixty"—Mr. Jackson had been making a Cabinet. Of course, he was to have his own
group of cronies as confidential advisers, his kitchen
Cabinet—Isaac Hill and editor Blair, nephew Donel-

son and Major Eaton, Martin Van Buren, "Prince
of Kinderhook, Arch Chancellor," Amos Kendall,
"Lord Scullion, the Emperor's favorite Cupbearer,"
and "Lord Lewis, the Groom of the Chambers"—but
still there must be an official Cabinet for state occasions.

And so, on February 26, it was announced. For
Secretary of State, "the guileless Van Buren," who
had served as electioneering manager during the campaign, and of whom, at the time, Mr. John Quincy
Adams had said that "he is now acting over the part
in the affairs of the Union which Aaron Burr performed in 1799 and 1800, and there is much resemblance of character, manners and even person between
the two men." But Mr. Jackson called him "the
guileless Van Buren." For Secretary of the
Treasury, Mr. Ingham. For Postmaster General,
Mr. Barry. For Attorney General, Mr. Berrien.
For Secretary of the Navy, Mr. Branch, who gave
dinners and was once referred to as "that miserable
old woman." And for Secretary of War, Major John
H. Eaton, because he was an old friend, and there
must be at least one old friend in the Cabinet.

It did not set the Potomac on fire. Mr. Cambrel-
ing might maintain that the "murmurings are now
pretty secret," although when Mrs. Livingston, Mrs.
Hayne, Mrs. Sargent and Mrs. McLane "hold one of
their caucuses, ye gods what a storm!" Yet the gen-

eral impression, except in the immediate circles of the gentlemen concerned, was that the new Cabinet represented "the millennium of the minnows." And the murmurings were not so secret either, at least not in the case of Major Eaton.

"Astonishment and disappointment filled the minds of friends and foes," Mrs. Smith observed. "Public opinion . . . will not allow of Gen'l Eaton holding a place which would bring his wife into society. . . . Everyone acknowledges Gen'l Eaton's talents and virtues—but his late unfortunate connection is an obstacle to his receiving a place of honor. . . . Oh woman, woman! The rumor of yesterday was that he was to have no place at home but be sent abroad —so it was added (though evidently only for the joke of it) that he was to be Minister to Hayti, that being the most proper court for her to reside in. . . . Everyone thinks there is great confusion and difficulty, mortification and disappointment at the Wigwam." Mr. Adams also had various observations to make. "The character of the woman was . . . notorious, so notorious that much opposition was made to the appointment of her husband. . . . The private morals of the country were deeply outraged by the appointment of Eaton to an office of Cabinet Minister. . . . But what could be expected from a President of the United States himself an adjudicated adulterer!"

Mr. Adams evidently did not take a charitable view of the Robards episode in Mr. Jackson's life.

There seemed to be considerable objection to Major Eaton's wife. . . .

4

She had been born in 1795—some said later— Margaret, but always Peggy, O'Neil; the daughter of an Irish tavern keeper in Washington, William O'Neil, and his wife, a "remarkably efficient woman" who enjoyed the friendship of Mrs. Jackson when she came to the city, and the continued confidence and regard of Mr. Jackson throughout his administration. The General had first known the O'Neils in Washington before it had become the national capital; he had renewed his acquaintance with them in 1819, and again in 1823, when he stayed at the O'Neil tavern. William O'Neil was a popular character, a genial host, a famous wit; his hostelry was the great resort of Congressmen and Senators. Major Eaton, Senator from Tennessee since 1818, spent all his winters there for ten years.

The first recorded appearance of Peggy in the national annals into which she was subsequently so conspicuously to intrude, occurred at the Union Tavern in Georgetown when she was a young girl, upon which occasion Mrs. President Madison had the pleasure of awarding to her the crown for the best exhibition of their art by the pupils of a dancing academy. The beginning and the end of Peggy's unusual career seem to have involved dancing masters. She was astonishingly pretty, lively, impudent and full of blarney. At her own tavern she was a public pet, a spoiled favorite of all the gentlemen, a little pitcher with very big ears, a broth of a girl with a tongue.

They sent her to school, to Mrs. Hayward's Seminary, and to Mr. Kirk's. Her sojourn at these academies must have added greatly to the gaiety of scholastic endeavor. At the age of fifteen, she left school and went back to her father's tavern—already a celebrated belle, the talk of the town, a young lady of unreticent charms whose conversation and deportment were not hampered by any unnecessary prudery— until, having become enamored of a certain Captain Root, she attempted to elope with him one night by climbing out of her window. An unsuccessful attempt, due to the sudden noisy disintegration of a flower pot which brought her father upon the scene. Mr. O'Neil was duly enraged, and packed her off to New York, where he put her to school again, at Mrs. Nau's, under the special supervision—if tradition is to be believed—of no less a personage than Mr. DeWitt Clinton. But the restrained decorum of Mrs. Nau's academy for young females, to say nothing of the barren formality of Mr. Clinton's establishment, were too much for Peggy. She begged and implored to be taken home, and the parental anger was finally soothed. There was probably a big time at the tavern when she returned. And then one day she looked out of her window and saw Mr. John Bowie Timberlake riding by. They were married in less than a month.

Mr. John Bowie Timberlake was a handsome gentleman who had seen service in the navy and was temporarily in business ashore. He was acquainted with Mr. Jackson, and a close friend of Major Eaton. The two of them, and Mr. O'Neil, were brother Masons. The Timberlakes settled down at the tavern and had, in due course of time, two daughters, Virginia and Margaret, and a son who died in infancy. Major Eaton was now also living at the tavern. And although subsequently Mr. Jackson stoutly maintained the falseness of such gossip—basing his opinion on his long standing knowledge of Major Eaton's character, on the circumstance that the Major and Mr. Timberlake were Masons, and on his personal, though brief, observation of the Timberlake menage —there went forth into the town the rumor that Mrs. Timberlake's virtue lacked that constancy which should have been its chief adornment, and that Major Eaton had had every opportunity to familiarize himself with this fact. It was more than a rumor, it was a conviction shared by the whole of Washington society.

The only person, apparently, who was not a beneficiary of this information, was Mr. Timberlake himself, although the point is by no means clear, and his attitude in the proceedings remains problematical. But at all events, his friendship for Major Eaton does not seem to have abated, and when, along in 1822, Mr. Timberlake returned to the navy as purser, it was the Major who acted as his bondsman. And now Mr. Timberlake was away frequently at sea, and the rumors increased. Some six years elapsed, and then one day, in 1828, it was learned that Mr. Timberlake had cut his throat at Port Mahon, aboard the frigate *Constitution*.

It was said, immediately, that the act had been caused by Mr. Timberlake's realization of his wife's infidelities—but Mr. Jackson insisted that this was ridiculous, since he had received a letter from Mr. Timberlake written only three weeks before his death, in which the latter had referred to Major Eaton as his dear friend. And there did seem to be another possible motive for the suicide, as the unfortunate Lieutenant Randolph who replaced Mr. Timberlake soon found out. For when the *Constitution* completed her cruise, the purser's accounts were seen to be in extremely dubious shape, and either Mr. Timberlake or Lieutenant Randolph was a defaulter.

And then a very curious series of events took place. The Timberlake accounts were sent in, and among them, Mr. Adams reports, were several letters from Major Eaton acknowledging the receipt of remit-

PEGGY EATON

From a portrait by Inman

Courtesy of the Robert Fridenberg Galleries

tances. But these had never been credited to Mr. Timberlake. The letters passed from Mr. Amos Kendall, who was fourth auditor of the Treasury, through various hands into those of Mr. Jackson. In the meantime, the court of enquiry acquitted Lieutenant Randolph of any blame. Whereupon, Mr. Kendall pressed the charges before the President, and Mr. Jackson dismissed Lieutenant Randolph from the service. The latter, very naturally, accused Mr. Jackson of having fastened the blame upon him in order to shield his friend, Major Eaton, who had been Mr. Timberlake's bondsman. It does appear as though a monumental injustice was done Mr. Randolph, whose only consolation was derived from such pleasure as he may have obtained in pulling Mr. Jackson's nose—a feat which he accomplished most successfully in 1833, in the cabin of a steamboat at Alexandria. The Senate had already had some extremely disagreeable things to say concerning Major Eaton's apparent connection with the Timberlake affairs, but Mr. Jackson and Mr. Kendall had settled the case to their own satisfaction, and the scandal blew over, as scandals will if sufficiently ignored. . . .

5

But Major Eaton had not finished with Mr. Timberlake's affairs. Not many months after his friend's death, the Major went to Mr. Jackson and announced

his intention of marrying the widow. Mr. Jackson
was delighted. Of course, the Major reminded him,
there had been rumors, rumors linking their names.
Then all the better if he married her, Mr. Jackson
told him, for it would "disprove these charges and
restore Peg's good name." And so, on January 1,
1829, they were married at Georgetown, and there
was "a great show of fashion and a Western frolic"
at the wedding—although one had better take the
show of fashion with a grain of salt.

Peggy was now a noted beauty; of medium height,
gracefully proportioned, famous for her Greek pro-
file, her wealth of dark hair curling about the wide
forehead, and the delicate loveliness of her pink and
white complexion. She was, in other respects, less
graceful, totally lacking in delicacy, and conspicuously unlovely. "Mrs. Eaton," Mr. Adams wrote,
"is as much a character as Van Buren." She had a
fearful temper, the conversational methods of a fish-
wife, and a habit of unbridled profanity. She was,
in the opinion of Mrs. Smith, "one of the most ambitious, violent, malignant, yet silly women you ever
heard of."

Washington was not pleased with the wedding.

"Tonight," Mrs. Smith, again, remarked, "Gen'l
Eaton, the bosom friend and almost adopted son of
Gen'l Jackson, is to be married to a lady whose repu-

tation her previous connection with him before and after her husband's death has totally destroyed. . . . She has never been admitted into good society, is very handsome and of not an inspiring character, and violent temper. She is, it is said, irresistible and carries whatever point she sets her mind on. The General's personal and political friends are very much disturbed about it; his enemies laugh and divert themselves with the idea of what a suitable lady in waiting Mrs. Eaton will make to Mrs. Jackson, and repeat the old adage 'birds of a feather will flock together.' "

The news of Mrs. Jackson's death had not yet reached Washington to quiet the infamous echoes of the old Robards slander. "The ladies declare they will not go to the wedding, and if they can help it will not let their husbands go."

But some of them did go, to take part in that "Western frolic."

January passed. People were speculating about the new Cabinet, and learning with dismay that there was question of including Major Eaton's name, when "the principal mischief maker," according to Mr. Adams, a "busybody" clergyman called Ezra Stiles Ely, came to Washington from Philadelphia on a visit to his colleague, the Reverend J. N. Campbell. Both men were Jackson supporters, and Mr. Campbell was pastor of the church in which Mrs. Jackson had worshipped during her stay in the capital. They talked. Mr. Ely told Mr. Campbell what he knew about Mrs. Eaton, and hoped that her husband would not be made a Cabinet officer. Mr. Campbell agreed with him, and told Mr. Ely what *he* knew. He had had it at first hand from a gentleman in Georgetown, since deceased, and it was not a story to shout from the housetops.

Mr. Ely went home to mull over these disclosures, and in a few weeks the Cabinet list containing the objectionable name was made public. Washington was deeply shocked, or at all events offended, and immediately made up its mind to have nothing to do with the scabrous lady. Even on Inauguration Day already, when the White House party attended in company with the Vice-President's lady, Mrs. Calhoun, Mrs. Ingham and the wives of two prominent Jacksonian Senators,

"this New Lady never approached the party. . . . She was left alone, and kept at a respectful distance from those virtuous and distinguished women, with the sole exception of a seat at the supper table, where, however, notwithstanding her proximity"—in a pink gown with black plumes—"she was not spoken to by them. These are . . . facts, greatly to the honor of our sex."

It was a lady, in this case, writing to her sister. But very soon it was the Reverend Ezra Stiles Ely writing to Mr. Jackson. . . .

6

The administration, consequently, was not three weeks old, before the President found himself face to face with the imbroglio which was to endure for three seasons. Mr. Ely had written to tell him a number of distressing facts concerning Mrs. Eaton which it is not necessary to enumerate in these pages, including the Georgetown story, and ventured to remind the President that Mrs. Jackson had had the worst opinion of Peggy.

Mr. Jackson replied at once, and at great length, in defense of the lady's reputation. He disposed of the various accusations as being ridiculous or "rumor, mere rumor." Mrs. Jackson had always considered Mrs. Eaton to be "an innocent and much injured woman." He had known Major Eaton for twenty years, and was he now to change his opinion of him "because of the slanders of this city? We know, here, that none are spared. Even Mrs. Madison was assailed by these fiends in human shape." He was "disgusted even to loathing at the licentious and depraved state of society." It needed purifying. The whole business had been trumped up by Mr. Clay and his friends. Mr. and Mrs. Clay had spoken "in the strongest and most unmeasured terms of Mrs. Eaton," who was actually "a much injured woman, and more virtuous than some of her enemies."

When she visited him, Mr. Jackson proposed to treat her—

"with as much politeness as I have ever done, believing her to be virtuous. . . . As to the determination of the ladies in Washington, I have nothing, nor will I ever have anything to do with it"—if only he had persevered in this attitude. "I will not persuade or dissuade any of them from visiting Mrs. Eaton, leaving Mrs. Eaton and them to settle the matter in their own way. On my nieces I lay no restriction. I only enjoin it on them to treat all well who may call to see them; they are required to visit none but those they may think proper."

And then, he observed to Mr. Ely—

"whilst on the one hand we should shun base women as a pestilence of the worst and most dangerous kind to society, we ought, on the other hand, to guard virtuous female character with vestal vigilance. Female virtue is like a tender and delicate flower; let but the breath of suspicion rest upon it, and it withers and perhaps perishes forever."

He was thinking, of course, of his wife, and of the revival of the Robards affair which had helped to kill her. "When it shall be assailed by envy and malice, the good and the pious will maintain its purity and innocence, until guilt is made manifest—not by rumors and suspicions, but by facts and proofs brought forth and sustained by respectable and fearless witnesses in the face of day."

It was an excellent letter, but Mr. Ely was not convinced and Mr. Jackson wrote again. The accusations were "vile slanders," and two ladies of Washington were responsible for them. In the meantime, Mr. Jackson began to collect affidavits and certificates of Mrs. Eaton's good character. If one came office seeking, it was well to bring along a certificate. Mr. Ely, for this part, allowed his views to become more widely known, and pretty soon Major Eaton was demanding explanations from Mr. Campbell. Mrs. Eaton went to Philadelphia and no doubt spoke her mind to Mr. Ely. The summer passed, and finally, on September 1, Mr. Campbell called on the President to support Mr. Ely, and in particular to corroborate the Georgetown episode. Mr. Jackson did not believe a word of it. Its significance depended on Mr. Timberlake's absence—when had it happened? Mr. Campbell said in 1821. Mr. Jackson examined Mr. Timberlake's books and found that he had been at home throughout the period under discussion. He then summond Mr. Campbell and advised him of this fact. Mr. Campbell insisted that Mr. Jackson had mistaken the date given him. Mr. Jackson then invited Mr. Campbell to give another date, which Mr. Campbell refused to do at the time.

On September 10, Mr. Ely also having been sent

for, Mr. Campbell was asked to appear at a Cabinet council, at which Mr. Jackson did most of the talking. After an opening dissertation on calumny, the question of the date came up again for acrimonious discussion. Mr. Campbell, who had consulted his informant's family, now decided that it should have been in 1826. Mr. Jackson would have none of it— Mr. Campbell had said 1821 before, and 1821 it must be, and in 1821 circumstances were such as to render the Georgetown gentleman's report laughable. Mr. Campbell had some dignified observations to make concerning the preservation of national morals from contamination, and withdrew after offering to support all his statements in a court of law. Mr. Ely admitted that the charges involving Major Eaton were apparently groundless, but refused to commit himself on Mrs. Eaton. Mr. Jackson insisted that she was "as chaste as a virgin." The Cabinet did not attempt to argue the point.

"Both Mr. Campbell and Dr. Ely," Mr. Jackson recorded, "acknowledged to me in the presence of my Cabinet, Mr. Van Buren, Mr. Ingham, Mr. Branch, Mr. Barry and Mr. Berrien, and also Major Lewis" —who appeared for Major Eaton—"and Major Donelson, that they entirely acquitted Major Eaton of the charge of improper or criminal conduct."

The case was closed.

7

But the case was not closed at all.   In spite of Mr. Jackson, society persisted in refusing to have anything to do with Peggy.

"As for the New Lady . . . after a thousand rumors and much tittle tattle, and gossip, and prophecyings, and apprehensions, public opinion ever just and impartial seems to have triumphed over personal feelings and intrigues, and finally doomed her to continue in her pristine lowly condition.   A stand, a noble stand . . . since it is a stand taken against power and favoritism, has been made by the ladies of Washington, and not even the President's wishes in favour of his dearest personal friend can influence them to violate the respect due to virtue by visiting one who has left her straight and narrow path.   With the exception of two or three timid and rather insignificant personages who trembled for their husbands' offices, not a lady has visited her, and so far from being inducted into the President's house she is . . . scarcely noticed by the females of his family."

Mr. Jackson did not know what to make of it.   He might put his foot down and issue pronunciamentos, but nothing could induce Mrs. Calhoun to change her attitude, and with her Mrs. Branch, Mrs, Ingham, Mrs. Berrien, Mrs. Huygens the Dutch Minister's wife, and the leaders of the Congressional and Senatorial sets. Their doors were closed to Mrs. Eaton, their carriages simply did not roll up her street. He might fulminate as much as he chose at home, but Mrs. Donelson would not lift a foot to visit Mrs. Eaton. It was the first time that anyone had successfully presumed to oppose his authority, to set aside his decisions, to ignore his commands. For the dictator of New Orleans and Pensacola, it was a mortifying and exasperating experience. These women!

And for the husband of the lamented Rachel Jackson, it was a fierce determination, a driving passion, a sacred cult, that Peggy Eaton be vindicated and exalted. They had slandered Rachel during the years of the campaign, they had driven her to her death finally with their infamous persecution, and "by the Eternal! The spiteful cats who plagued the life out of my patient Rachel shall not scratch this brave little Peggy!" Brave little Peggy was an angel, a woman in distress, a victim of calumny and falsehood. The bereaved, obstinate, chivalrous old man at the White House could see in her nothing but the embodiment of his Rachel's virtues, the expression of his Rachel's sorrows. The Cabinet, society in general, must be forced to receive her, to disavow past judgments, to do homage to her—and through her to the memory of Rachel Jackson. Peggy was actually little more than a symbol, the guerdon of a relentless revenge; for three years it was from a grave in a Ten-

nessee garden that many pages of American history
were dictated.

At the same time, Mr. Jackson was not entirely
unsupported in his stand against the community.
There were some who took sides with Peggy—gentlemen for the most part, it must be noted—Major
Lewis, of course, who was a brother-in-law of Major
Eaton; Mr. Vaughan and Baron Krudener, the British and Russian Ministers, two lively bachelors who
could afford a broad-minded charity which cost them
nothing; Mr. Barry, who meant to retain his post in
the Cabinet and did so and Mr. Van Buren. "Calhoun leads the moral party," Mr. Adams remarked,
"Van Buren that of the frail sisterhood." The guileless Van Buren was a widower, he was the little friend
of all the universe, the great pourer of oil on troubled
waters; he had nothing to lose and perhaps, as may
become apparent, everything in the world to gain.

He went out of his way—but the longest detour is
sometimes the shortest route—to be nice to Peggy.
It was he who persuaded those complaisant diplomats,
Ministers Vaughan and Krudener, to lend their social
prestige to Peggy's cause; it was he who took Mrs.
Donelson to the table at that first dreadful Cabinet
dinner at the White House in November, that
"formal and hollow ceremony" which all his tact and
good humor could not rescue from frigid disaster; it
was he who arranged those charming parties for

Peggy, which always began so pleasantly and ended so uncomfortably in spite of the best intentions. In fact, "if Mr. Van Buren, our Secretary, persists in visiting her our ladies will not go to his house." But he did persist, and continue to arrange parties—for was he not the guileless Van Buren?

A formal banquet, for instance, announced so guilelessly in honor of Mr. Jefferson's daughter, Mrs. Randolph, so that it was difficult to refuse. But the Berriens were out of town, and Mrs. Branch and Mrs. Ingham were indisposed. A splendid ball of Mr. Vaughan's, opened by the Secretary of the Legation and Mrs. Eaton—only when they stood up for the cotillion all the other couples in the set disappeared. Another great ball given by Baron Krudener—they took it in turns—at which it was planned to have the Baron escort Mrs. Eaton in to supper while Major Eaton did the honors for Mrs. Huygens of the Dutch Legation; but it did not work out that way, for when Mrs. Huygens discovered the fact that she was to sit at the same table with the "upstart" she seized her own husband's arm and marched him swiftly, however reluctantly, out of the house.

"Mrs. Eaton continues excluded from society," Mrs. Smith reports, "except the houses of some of the foreigners, the President's and Mr. V.B.'s. The Dutch Minister's family have openly declared against her admission into society. The other evening . . .

at the Russian Minister's, Mrs. E. was led first to
the supper table, in consequence of which Mrs.
Madm. Heugans and family would not go to the
table and was quite enraged—for the whole week you
heard of scarcely anything else."

The Eaton Malaria, as Mr. Van Buren called it,
was entering upon its most virulent stages.

8

Of course, Mr. Van Buren knew exactly what he
was doing.

"The Eaton imbroglio," he himself explained it; "a
private and personal matter which only acquired political consequences by its adaptation to the gratification of resentments springing out of the formation of
the Cabinet, and, as was supposed, to the elevation or
depression of individuals of high position."

Quite so. Mr. Jackson was, for the time being Czar
of all the Americas, he was the dispenser of political
good fortune, he would, presumably, have much to
say concerning the choice of his successor. Even so
guileless a person as Mr. Van Buren could not long
remain unaware of the fact that the avenue of approach to Mr. Jackson's favor was open only to those
who earned his esteem by a diligent blowing of Peggy
Eaton's horn. Mr. Van Buren did not hesitate to
become her Little Boy Blue. Mr. Adams was quite
prepared to hit the nail on the head. Mr. Van Buren,

he said, "is notoriously engaged in canvassing for the presidency by paying his court to Mrs. Eaton. He uses personal influence with the wives of his partisans to prevail upon them to countenance this woman by visiting her." He even tried it on Mrs. Donelson, with singular ill success since all he obtained from her was a statement that, in her opinion, *honesty* was the best policy.

Everyone understood what was going on, except the deluded old gentleman at the White House who was so fond of his Marty.

"Mr. Van Buren has evidently, at this moment, quite the lead in influence and importance," Mr. Webster admitted. "He controls all the pages on the back stairs, and flatters what seems to be at present the Aaron's serpent among the President's desires, a settled purpose of making out the lady of whom so much has been said a person of reputation. It is odd enough, but too evident to be doubted, that the consequence of this dispute in the social and fashionable world is producing great political effects, and may very probably determine who shall be successor to the present Chief Magistrate."

The Calhouns, for instance, if they entertained any hopes of achieving the presidency, were going about it in the worst possible way. And Mr. Van Buren was not liable to lose any sleep over a political disaster to Mr. Calhoun.

Mrs. Smith, also, saw which way the wind was blowing.

"Our government is becoming every day more and more democratic, the rulers of the people are truly their servants, and among those rulers women are gaining more and more than their share of power," she observed, with her tongue in her cheek. "One woman has made sad work here; to be, or not to be, her friend is the test of presidential favor. Mr. V. B. sided with her and is consequently the right hand man, the constant riding, walking and visiting companion . . . while the other members of the Cabinet are looked on coldly, some say unkindly, and enjoy little share in the councils of state."

Only it was not Peggy doing all this, really—it was Rachel Jackson. . . .

One does not know what Peggy thought of it all. She was ambitious, proud, vindictive; she probably enjoyed the battle and fought it with all her heart and with all her wits. Bellona, they sometimes called her in the newspapers. Her good spirits never failed her, they say, and she was always regaling her friends with humorous descriptions and mimicries of the scenes of her repeated discomfitures. Maybe so. One can only speculate upon the depths of her private mortifications. She was, one imagines, a very shallow person. It would not have occurred to her that she was merely a piece in Mr. Van Buren's political

game of checkers, to be moved about on the board
where it would be most likely to annoy Mr. Calhoun.
And she had her triumphs; she was "the Pompadour,"
she was "Her Immaculate Highness, Rosilia, Princess of Influence," men came to her with gifts—there
is a curious reference to canaries—seeking largesse
from the "Emperor."

And already in December, 1829, Mr. Jackson had
settled on Mr. Van Buren for the next presidency,
and was writing confidential communications on behalf of the "Little Magician."

9

But in 1830, for a while at least, the lady who was
causing all the trouble was—

"forced, notwithstanding the support and favor of
such high personages, to withdraw from society. She
is not received in any private parties, and since the
8th of January has withdrawn from public assemblies.
At the ball given on that occasion she was treated with
such marked and universal neglect and indignity that
she will not expose herself again to such treatment.
Gen'l E. unable to clear his wife's fair name, has
taken his revenge by blackening that of other ladies."

All the members of Congress were "full of rumors
respecting the volcanic state of the administration."
The Reverend Ezra Stiles Ely had been called to

THE PRESIDENT'S HOUSE IN 1831

From an engraving published in 1831 by Hinton, Simpkin & Marshall

Washington again as mediator, but had accomplished
nothing. The President, Mr. Adams thought in February, had been ready to dismiss Mr. Branch, but had
been informed that in such an event Mr. Ingham and
Mr. Berrien would also resign.

"He concluded, therefore, to retain Mr. Branch, and
became a mediator between him and Eaton. . . . Ingham, Branch, Berrien, Towson have given large evening parties to which Mrs. Eaton is not invited. On
the other hand, the President makes her doubly conspicuous by an over display of notice. At the last
drawing room . . . she had a crowd gathered around
her and was made the public gaze. But Mrs. Donelson . . . held no conversation with her. The administration party is split up into a blue and a green
faction . . . but the explosion has been hitherto de-
ferred."

Mr. Adams did not know it at the time, but there
had already been an explosion in January. It all came
out much later in the newspapers, in the *Telegraph*
and in the *Globe*, in a tempest of statements, and
accusations, and denials which rendered it almost impossible, in 1831, to ascertain just what everyone
actually had done or said at the moment. Whether
Congressman Johnson came as an emissary to Mr.
Ingham and his friends with threats of dismissal unless they invited Mrs. Eaton to their parties, and if
so, whether he said that Mr. Jackson was like a roar-

ing lion and believed that "Mrs. Huygens . . . had joined in the conspiracy against Mrs. Eaton, and that he would send Huygens home to teach him . . . that the wife of a member of his Cabinet should not be treated so." Whether the Secretaries had a paper read to them by the President informing them that if a combination existed against Major Eaton "it would be considered of," or whether the interview was merely conversational. Mr. Berrien, corroborated by Mr. Branch and Mr. Ingham, admitted the interview but denied the reading of any document. Mr. Blair, of the *Globe* —Mr. Jackson's "Bla'r"—was insultingly positive about the document. Everybody got very red in the face in 1831.

But in January, 1830, a few days after the event, Mr. Jackson—who had a way of annotating himself for posterity—drew up a memorandum describing the interview, the veracity of which one may not presume to doubt. He had been told of the existence of a combination to drive Major Eaton from the Cabinet, and so he had sent for Mr. Ingham, Mr. Branch and Mr. Berrien.

"I informed them," he stated, "of the information I had recd . . . from the members of Congress, and that I had sent for them for explanation and enquiry whether the information . . . was correct. When we met I read them the following statement—

"The Personal difficulties between some of the

members of my Cabinet have assumed an aspect and
received a bearing in regard to myself which requires
an expression of my personal feelings. To prevent
future misunderstandings I have deemed it exped-
ient to have this interview with Mr. Ingham, Mr.
Branch and Mr. Berrien. When we met I said to
them . . . that the course pursued by them to Major
Eaton and his family as reported to me, was in my
opinion, under the circumstances not only unjust in
itself but disrespectful to myself. . . . I do not
claim the right to interfere in any manner in the domestic relations or personal intercourse of any member of my Cabinet. . . . But . . . I am fully im-
pressed with a belief that you and your families, have
in addition to the exercise of their own undoubted
rights in this respect taken measures to induce others
to avoid intercourse with Mrs. Eaton and thereby
sought to exclude her from society. . . . " He had,
he explained, himself chosen Major Eaton and continued him in the Cabinet in spite of malicious slanders against Mrs. Eaton, and therefore—

"If her character is such as to justify active measures on the part of the members of my Cabinet to exclude her from virtuous society it is I who am responsible to the community for this alledged indignity to
the public morals. I will not part with Major Eaton
from my Cabinet and those of my Cabinet who cannot harmonize with it had better withdraw, for harmony I must and will have. . . . Therefore have I
sought this interview to assure you that if there be
any truth in the report that you have entered into the
combination charged . . . that I feel it an indignity

and insult offered to myself, and is of a character
that will remain hereafter to be condemned."

The paper may, at that, have been merely the notes
from which he talked to them, and part of it, certainly, would seem to have been written after the
interview; but it was endorsed by Mr. Jackson as follows—"This was read to them, and being informed by
the gentlemen that as far as their influence went, it
was exercised differently, and their wish was to har-
monise the Cabinet, I determined not to dismiss
them." The Secretaries went home and found their
wives waiting for them, no doubt, on the doorstep;
and once again, in Mr. Jackson's estimation, the case
was closed. . . .

10

He hoped that they would let him alone now with
their bickerings; that they would all be nice to Mrs.
Eaton, and leave him to a little peace, a little quiet
enjoyment of his White House. And as the rigors
of mourning for Mrs. Jackson began to be relaxed,
the White House was not at all an unpleasant place.
The stateliness, the *savoir faire,* the social refinements
of previous administrations were lacking, but there
was a kindly simplicity of manners, a comfortable,
firelit atmosphere of domestic living, which were most
attractive. Young Mrs. Jackson was delightful,
everyone was devoted to Mrs. Donelson, in time the

big formal rooms were almost always filled with the agreeable clamor of romping children. Mr. Jackson gave excellent dinners—although he himself could scarcely ever eat anything except bread and milk and vegetables—plentifully furnished with fine dishes and choice wines. Fifty or sixty pounds of meat a day was an average White House order, and there were months when its cellar provided eighteen bottles of London porter and French wine, three barrels of ale and beer and twelve gallons of brandy, Holland gin and Jamaica spirits.

Of course, the levees were extremely "republican." They were, during the second administration, to become quite brilliant; well ordered functions at which hundreds of guests—among them bevies of ladies in satin and velvet—were treated to ices, jellies and wines; but in the opening years they were still very much the resort of the yahoos.

"The old man stood in the centre of a little circle," Mr. Bancroft reported in 1831, "and shook hands with everybody that offered. The number of ladies who attended was small; nor were they brilliant. But to compensate for it there was a throng of apprentices, boys of all ages, men not civilised enough to walk about the room with their hats off; the vilest, promiscuous medley that ever was congregated in a decent house; many of the lowest gathering round the doors, pouncing with avidity upon the wine and refreshments, tearing the cake with the ravenous keenness of intense hunger; starvelings, and fellows with dirty faces and dirty manners; all the refuse that Washington could turn forth from its workshops and stables."

Something which Mr. Van Buren, who put Corinthian Oil of Cream and Concentrated Extract of Eglantine on his person, was not to permit during his administration. But still, it would all have been very cheerful and homelike, if only the Eaton case had really been closed.

But it was not closed. The ladies of the Cabinet were not inviting Peggy to their parties; Mrs. Calhoun and Mrs. Huygens had not changed their minds; the three Lotharios were not having any better success with their dinners and balls; Mrs. Donelson refused to visit the Princess Rosilia. The Malaria was still raging. And very soon Mr. Jackson was raging, and to considerable purpose. "President Jackson," Mr. Adams wrote in March, "has forced Mrs. Donelson . . . to visit Mrs. Eaton and to invite her to the christening of her child, to which Mr. Van Buren stood sponsor and Miss Cora Livingston godmother."

It was a triumph for Peggy; but it was dearly bought at the White House, for Mrs. Donelson told her uncle that if she was to be obliged henceforth to visit the lady she would go back to Tennessee. Mr.

Jackson chose to make it a test of his authority, and in the spring the Donelsons went home, not to return until the fall of 1831. The Pompadour's influence had achieved its first banishment from the Court. Mr. Jackson was mortally hurt by his niece's desertion, but he did not relent and during the summer of 1830 he took his revenge and gave Peggy her second triumph. The Eatons were in Tennessee, they were coming to Nashville, and Nashville society was preparing an array of cold shoulders. Mr. Jackson immediately invited them to the Hermitage, and not only that, but he managed to gather all the Donelsons around him when they arrived, including the rebellious Emily. "My neighbours and connections," he wrote Major Eaton, "will receive you and your Lady with that good feeling which is due to you, and I request you and your Lady will meet them with your usual courtesy." Yes. It was probably the greatest victory in the General's whole career. On paper.

But things could not go on as they were. Society was disgruntled and hostile; the Cabinet was split; Congress was beginning to complain, as it assembled for the session of 1831. Washington was hearing entirely too much about Bellona. And perhaps Mr. Van Buren was tired of giving parties for her, or else the time had come to abandon a scene grown finally too complex for his guileless nature. In any case,

Mr. Calhoun was now no longer a serious presidential rival. At all events, the Little Magician summoned forth all his wizardry. . . .

11

He decided to resign from the Cabinet. The trick, of course, was to get Major Eaton to resign, in order to restore harmony to the councils of the Democratic party—if it was to remain in power and give Mr. Van Buren his turn. And anyway, Mr. Van Buren's resignation was also a necessary step in his career, since Mr. Jackson had laid down the law that no active member of his Cabinet might consider himself a presidential candidate. In his daily rides with the President, Mr. Van Buren gradually approached the subject. No mention was made of Major Eaton; Mr. Van Buren took all the blame on himself—the whole present entanglement was due to him; he was the *persona* most *non grata* in hostile, official circles; he must go. Yes, the post of Minister to Great Britain would do very nicely—of course Mr. Jackson must realize that some day—well—yes. It was all very noble and guileless.

They rode and talked for several days, and then Mr. Van Buren gave one of his pleasant little dinners for Mr. Jackson, Mr. Barry, Major Lewis and Major Eaton. Mr. Van Buren's intention of resigning —of offering himself up for the sake of harmony—

MARTIN VAN BUREN

From an engraving of a portrait by Inman

was announced, and Major Eaton immediately did what Mr. Van Buren had hoped he would do. Mr. Van Buren wanted to know how Mrs. Eaton would view her husband's resignation, and Major Eaton was sure that she would agree. Mr. Jackson was willing. One gets the impression that all these champions were just a little weary, now, of the Eaton Malaria, and ready to accept any satisfactory cure. They met again the next evening, and Major Eaton reported that his wife had consented; although her very "cold and formal" reception of Mr. Jackson and Mr. Van Buren a short time later seemed to indicate that her consent was only verbal. One ventures to suggest that Major Eaton—who cannot have been enjoying himself all these months—probably made it clear to Peggy that her Cabinet days were over, whether she liked it or not.

And so the resignations were arranged. Major Eaton sent his in on April 7, 1831, Mr. Van Buren his on April 11, Mr. Jackson having insisted on that order. They were accepted, and Mr. Jackson promptly notified Mr. Berrien, Mr. Ingham and Mr. Branch that he wished to effect a general reorganization of his official entourage. They resigned at once, on April 18 and 19. The faithful Mr. Barry alone remained, and Mr. Adams noted that "not a human being of any party regrets the loss of the services of any of the Secretaries withdrawn." Peggy had lost her

place, but three other ladies had been expelled, a rea-
sonably adequate sacrifice to her pride.

Of course, the dissolution of the Cabinet made an
enormous sensation, increased in a few weeks by the
publication in the newspapers of the controversies,
already referred to, between Mr. Blair and the Secretaries. For the first time, people in general realized
how strongly Peggy's destinies had influenced those
of the administration; although some hint of it had
been conveyed in the airing of a ridiculous brawl between Major Eaton and Mr. Ingham, during the
course of which the latter complained to Mr. Jackson
that the Major and his friends had tried to murder
him. They had waylaid him, he insisted, "for the
purpose of assassination." Maybe so; at all events,
Mr. Ingham had suddenly departed—reserving for
himself, so it was said, all the seats in the Baltimore
coach—leaving the enraged Major to stew in his own
grease.

So, in the midst of considerable merriment, the
"millennium of the minnows" came to an end, in a
tempest of undignified billingsgate. Mr. Van Buren
having washed his hands of the whole affair, dried
them, and prepared to pass over his Department to
Mr. Edward Livingston; Mr. Calhoun plunged
headlong into Nullification; Mr. Jackson returned
to his Bank.

12

Peggy had scored a considerable triumph, if she
chose to consider it so—and in Nashville that autumn
the ladies came flocking to visit her under Mr. Jackson's sternly compelling eye—but she was not satisfied. Not even when the President arranged for the
recall of Mr. Huygens, that is to say of Mrs. Huygens, as a final offering to her vanity. The newspapers, Mrs. Smith thought, were not exaggerating,
"nay, do not detail one half of his imbecilities. He is
completely under the government of Mrs. Eaton.
. . . You will soon see the recall of the Dutch Ministry announced. Madm. Huygens' spirited conduct
in refusing to visit Mrs. E. is undoubtedly the
cause."

But Peggy would not abandon the battlefield.

"It was hoped, on her husband's going out of office,
she would have left the city, but she will not. . . . Mrs.
E. can not be forced or persuaded to leave Washington. Her triumph, for so she calls the dissolution
of the Cabinet, her triumph, she says, is not yet complete. All her adversaries are not yet turned out of
office; to be sure three secretaries and a foreign minister are dismissed, but Mr. and Mr. and Mr. remain,
they too must go, and she must be received into society, and she hopes and believes that next winter the
present Cabinet ministers will open their doors for
her."

In fact, it was supposed that if the new Cabinet did
not yield on this point it would soon be dismissed.
"Several of them in order to avoid this dilemma are
determined not to keep house or bring on their families. . . . Our society is in a bad state. Intrigues
and parasites in favor, divisions and animosity exist-
ing. . . . "

But society had no intention of substantiating
Peggy's rather hollow victory, and in the meantime,
something must be found for Major Eaton in com-
pensation for his post. It had been hoped that he
might become Senator from Tennessee again, but in
spite of Mr. Jackson's active efforts he was defeated
for the office. Tennessee might visit his wife, but it
would not select him as its representative. And so,
in 1834, Mr. Jackson made him Governor of Florida,
and for two years Peggy ruled such society as was to
be found in Pensacola.

And now it was the Major who was not satisfied;
Pensacola was no place in his estimation—nor, probably in Peggy's—and he kept clamoring for a more
important position until, in 1836, just as Mr. Van
Buren was preparing to reap the fruit of his magic,
they appointed him Minister to Spain. That was
much better. Peggy was extremely beautiful and
enormously witty, the Major was wealthy, on the
packet crossing the Atlantic Mrs. Eaton and the two
Timberlake daughters were "the life of the party."

Madrid knew nothing of O'Neil's tavern, or of the Timberlake affair, or of Bellona. The Reverend Ezra Stiles Ely did not visit Spain. The Spanish *beau monde* was delighted with Peggy, she became a favorite of the Queen, her daughter Virginia married a duke and went to live in France; for four years Peggy had the time of her life, she was a belle, a great lady, a privileged member of the proudest society in Europe. It was a curious social paradox, very similar to that exhibited in the case of Madame Jumel, who, after years of ostracism in New York, had found herself, not so long before, the sensation of Paris.

At all events, it was a real triumph, this time, for Peggy. Of course, one has no means of knowing how often *Señora* Eaton looked at the Queen of Spain and wished she were Mrs. Calhoun; nor does one feel competent to decide whether the joke was at the expense of Madrid or of Washington. . . .

13

One almost wishes that one might leave Peggy in Spain, under a mantilla of decorous respectability; but the facts do not permit so amenable a conclusion. There is the dancing master.

The Eatons returned to Washington in 1840, in time to allow Major Eaton—who for some reason had always objected to Mr. Van Buren—to campaign against the latter's re-election and join hands, consequently, with the enemies of Mr. Jackson. It was, under the circumstances, a peculiarly conspicuous display of ingratitude, and Mr. Jackson did not hesitate to proclaim his old friend "the most degraded of all the apostates fed, clothed and cherished by the administration." For sixteen years Major Eaton lived to think over those words, and then he died, on November 17, 1856. Peggy was sixty-one years old, the Major had left her a great deal of money, she was still, in spite of advancing years, quite strikingly beautiful. After Madrid, the enmities of Washington must have seemed fairly insignificant. She settled there, in considerable state and luxury; the orphan children of her other daughter were brought to live with her; there were plenty of people, no doubt, willing to come and visit the fascinating, wealthy dowager.

At all events, there was a dancing master, an Italian worthy who taught Peggy's grandchildren at Marini's academy. In the light of subsequent events it is a question whether actually he came to see Peggy or her beautiful granddaughter. But he came, and made the most of his opportunities; for one day, to everyone's astonishment, Peggy, who should really have known better at her age, married him. The comedy—if the spectacle of almost septuagenarian folly can be considered—soon turned to tragedy, however; for in a few days the bridegroom, having filled his pockets with Peggy's jewelry and as much of her money as he had been able to transfer into his keeping, abandoned his doting bride, and promptly eloped with the granddaughter!

This engaging pair sought shelter in Europe, found their way back to Montreal and eventually to New York. Peggy was left alone in Washington, deserted, impoverished, and pathetically ridiculous. There must have come to her, suddenly, a great disgust with life as she had known it, a vast resentment against the futility of her ambitions, an utter weariness of the shams of her distorted existence. Fate had only meant her to be a tavern keeper's daughter. Of course, there were always those four tremendous seasons in Spain to give Fate the lie.

She died on November 8, 1879, in her eighty-fourth year. What a dance it had been—Mr. Timberlake, Major Eaton, Baron Krudener, Mr. Van Buren, Mrs. Huygens, Mrs. Calhoun, Mr. Jackson, the Queen of Spain—but its most hateful echoes, surely, were those of the dancing master's fiddling. . . .